Peter Pindar's Poems

Peter Pindar's Poems

SELECTED BY P. M. ZALL

With a Foreword by A. L. Rowse

University of South Carolina Press
Columbia, South Carolina

This edition first published in Great Britain in 1972 for
Social Documents Ltd. by Adams & Dart
Bath, Somerset
and in the United States of America by the
University of South Carolina Press
Columbia, South Carolina

International Standard Book Number: 0-87249-251-6
Library of Congress Catalog Card Number: 72-178016

Suggested Library of Congress classification furnished by
McKissick Memorial Library of the University of South Carolina:
PR3765.W7A6
Manufactured in Great Britain

Contents

FOREWORD	*page* vii
INTRODUCTION	1
PETER'S APOLOGY	5
STORY: THE CORNISH LASSES	5
PERIPATETIC RAZOR-SELLER	6
PILGRIMS AND PEAS	8
EPISTLE TO JAMES BOSWELL	11
BOZZY AND PIOZZI	18
SIR JOSHUA REYNOLDS	29
ODE IX	30
APPLE DUMPLINGS AND A KING	32
BIRTH-DAY ODE	34
SOLOMON AND THE MOUSETRAP	41
SIR JOSEPH BANKS	46
THE KNIGHT AND THE RATS	49
STORY THE SECOND	50
FROGS AND JUPITER	51
OLD SIMON	53
THE WIDOW OF EPHESUS	57
ODE TO TWO MICE IN A TRAP	62
ODE ON THE CHOLERIC CHARACTER	63
TOPER AND THE FLIES	63
BALLADE TO A FISH OF THE BROOKE	65
THE YOUNG CROWS AND THE YOUNG WRENS	65
HYMN TO ADVERSITY	67
ELEGY	69

Foreword

Peter Pindar has always been a congenial name to me, if only because of all that he did to befriend and launch John Opie, the one Cornish painter of genius. But he was a significant and interesting figure in political, artistic and literary society in his own right during the reign of George III. He was, in fact, the chief satirist of the time in verse—an age that appreciated verse much as ours appreciates television. And George III was his chief subject, a constant target for Peter Pindar's wit and comic description of the King's eccentricities and mannerisms, his oddities of speech. As Peter candidly confessed: 'The King has been a good subject to me, but I have been a bad subject to his Majesty.'

That thought may make us wonder whether in some ways there was not more freedom, at any rate less tedious adherence to middle-class convention, in an aristocratic society than in our own. It is also a pointed comment on our age that where the Regency could sport a gifted versifier, a variegated comic wit like Peter, our own supports a pedestrian Muggeridge.

Peter Pindar's fame in his own day was something difficult for us to realise: seven or ten editions in a year of his burlesques and lampoons, the booksellers falling over each other to print his works. When Haydn appeared in London, Peter was called on to write the libretto of his oratorio The Storm. *And when the Polish patriot Kosciusko was in prison in St Petersburg, his jailer lent him a volume of Peter's works.* There *was fame!*

Actually Peter Pindar's real name was John Wolcot, and he was a Devonshire-man though he spent a number of earlier years in Cornwall. It was there while engaged as a doctor in Truro that he came across the mine-carpenter's boy, John Opie, who proved to have genius as a painter. Dr Wolcot took him into his house, taught him all that he himself had learned from Richard Wilson—the Doctor was a talented amateur artist—and eventually launched the 'Cornish Wonder' upon a somewhat astonished and much impressed London.

Opie's success was the result of the Doctor's carefully considered campaign, his subsequent fame the reward of his own genius and intense hard work. But the move to London came not a moment too soon. Dr Wolcot had long been ambitious to make a career for himself in the capital, and was understandably discontented with and irritated by the petty pomposities of the local figures in small-town society in Truro. They provided his first targets; but he was after bigger game, and the move to London provided it plentifully. There were celebrities like Boswell and Dr Johnson, there were the Royal Academicians, there were politicians, above all there was George III and his German Court with its comic ways. In short, unknown Dr Wolcot became famous Peter Pindar.

No-one was immune from his satire; and people were surprised when this satirist of the king turned his pen against the revolutionary, Tom Paine. (Left Intellectuals may deride everybody else, but they can't take being laughed at themselves.) Everyone must sympathise with Peter's making fun of solemn Hannah More, with her campaign for expurgating the poets on account of the harm they might do the youthful (female) mind.

It is interesting to observe the reaction of leading figures in the age to Peter's exposures. The stuffy Coleridge who, in spite of his own bad habits, was apt to be censorious about others, said, 'I swear to you that my flesh creeps at his name!' It is much to the credit of Wordsworth that he wrote, somewhat too enthusiastically: 'Boileau and Pope and the redoubted Peter: these are great names.' With Robert Burns, he was 'a first favourite of mine and a delightful fellow.' It was more difficult to please the discriminating Beckford; but he paid him a considerable tribute: 'How well he wrote, how original his style and talents; he understood character thoroughly, he played with human foibles.'

With that judgment in mind we may be assured that Peter is worth reading. But not, at this date, in full. I have long wanted a selection to introduce us to the best of his work. And Professor Paul Zall has given us just that. We may derive from it both pleasure and profit: pleasure and amusement in the verbal and metrical dexterity of this old popular master; while at the same time a portrait of his age, its foibles and audacities, its characters and caricatures, builds up, brush-stroke by stroke, in our minds. It may be hoped, then, that this judicious and representative selection may appeal and be of use to students of both English literature and history.

A. L. ROWSE

Introduction

A tale popular in 1800 tells about the Duke of Kent touring backwoods America and coming upon a little girl thoroughly engrossed in a book. 'What do you read, my dear?' says he. 'Sir,' she replies, 'the *Bible* and Peter Pindar.' The point of the joke is of course lost to modern readers, few of whom have ever heard of Peter Pindar. Parents of little girls in 1800, however, knew of him as a scurrilous satirist whose jingling gossip had titillated backstairs Britain for twenty years. It is quite possible that little girls could have read selections of his poems with only minimal risk, since Peter produced hundreds of harmless metrical tales about country bumpkins and peripatetic salesmen. Still, the bulk of his voluminous verse consisted rather of bawdy jests and scurrilous gossip as timely as the morning papers and produced with no care for polish or accuracy. Peter tossed off his poems with rapidity, fluidity, and buffoonish disregard for any standard, moral or aesthetic. His public loved him for it.

Peter Pindar, as the name suggests, was a fiction. He was a persona created by Dr John Wolcot, long-lived (1738–1819) Devonshireman, clergyman, physician, art critic, journalist—a virtuoso in the grand tradition who launched his first assault on the flanks of the fine arts in 1780 after having preached in Jamaica and practised medicine in Cornwall. Establishing camp in a London garret, Dr Wolcot let it be known that he had found a young Cornish lad drawing pictures on the banks of a clay pit, truly an original genius who had never before seen a painting, yet whose own paintings were now available for public viewing, under the patronage of Sir Joshua Reynolds, President of the Royal Academy, and a Devonshire man himself. Wolcot dressed young John Opie in a green hat with a long plume, a master touch ensuring the adulation of fashionable art lovers, who swirled through the garret and swept the young painter to fortune, fame, and marriage with a highly successful female novelist.

In addition to creating Opie in the image of original genius, or 'the Cornish Wonder,' Dr Wolcot created an image for himself as Peter Pindar. An habitual versifier, he had long composed poems for all occasions, social, political, historical, for the provincial press. He now turned his hobby into a trade. As an initial investment, he paid for the publication of an anonymous verse satire (written by himself) announcing Peter's arrival on the scene. The next year, 1782, he once again (but for the last time) paid to print the first in a series of 'Lyric Odes to the Royal Academicians'. The series gained wide popularity, appearing annually for five years, then intermittently until Dr Wolcot's death. The 'odes' were innovative in offering art criticism cloaked in uninhibited buffoonery:

And now, O Muse, with song so big,
Turn round to Gainsborough's Girl and Pig,
Or Pig and Girl I rather should have said:
The Pig in white, I must allow,
Is really a well-painted Sow;
I wish to say the same thing of the Maid.

Gratuitously, Peter included little metrical tales inserted at random among such critiques, some illustrating a point, others thrown in out of sheer exuberance. The result was a satura, or mixed dish, of art criticism, old jokes, folk tales, and current gossip, all garnished with a lively rhythm and jocular rhymes, foretelling of Byron's *Don Juan*.

Surely an important factor contributing to Peter's popular success was his choice of George III as target. The first of the 'Lyric Odes' commented slyly on the King's conservative taste in painting. The second commented more boldly on the King's misplacing patronage on unworthy painters. Intentionally or not, Peter had found his best subject, and his career thereafter rose and fell inversely with the popularity of George III. Occasionally Peter broadened his aim to include literary parody, mocking James Boswell in *Epistle to Boswell* (1786) and both Boswell and Mrs Piozzi in *Bozzy and Piozzi* (1786). But even in such literary satires Peter seldom wandered far from George III. Amidst his japes at the expense of Bozzy and Piozzi (chiefly versified from their own books), he would warn them repeatedly about potential competition from a local monarch, no mean gossiper himself.

In a natural progression, Peter combined both literary and political interests in a new series of odes addressed to incumbent poets laureate and other public figures who enjoyed royal patronage, including scientists such as Sir Joseph Banks, President of the Royal Society. Still, his favourite focal point centred in the mad antics of 'the best of Kings'. Everyone agreed that Peter looked elsewhere for his targets whenever the King suffered periods of actual madness. By keeping a clear distinction between satire of the monarch and subversion of the monarchy, Peter escaped arrest for libel and treason over the course of twenty-five years. His chief defence, of course, was that the material he used was common knowledge. Wild rumours circulated to the effect that Peter maintained hired spies in the King's household, and Peter encouraged such notoriety. But most of his material was readily available in the columns of the daily newspapers. Peter simply added versification.

With the French Revolution and the subsequent war between France and England, Peter's popularity suffered in proportion as reverence (and anxiety) for the King increased. Peter's buffoonery took on a self-consciously defensive air, then a strong Whiggish cast, as though trying to justify his satire as politically rather than commercially inspired. Members of the Government began to appear more frequently in his satires, especially the Prime Minister, 'Bottomless Pitt', particularly when public opinion raged against Pitt's raising taxes to pay for the war at a time when bad harvests and inflation spread misery across the land. Cries of 'Bread, No Pitt!' and then 'Bread, No King!' echoed in the cities, in 1795, and Peter's poems rose in popularity accordingly. But as British forces began to achieve victories in Europe and good harvests returned—and the Government imposed restrictions on press and public speeches—King George became the rallying point for a resurgence of patriotic feeling. As a contemporary observed, Peter's sun was setting, never to rise again (though he was to live on for another dozen years).

Dr Wolcot, in turn, became the object of scurrilous attack by defenders of King and Country and the legion of enemies who had earlier smarted under Peter's lash. As time passed, he became such a national butt that, at the age of 70, he was carried into court on a charge of adultery levied by a pair of lowest-class confidence men. The charge was dismissed, for it was obvious that Dr Wolcot was blind, infirm, and racked with asthma. Added to such illness was the pain incurred from dozens of writers who published outrageous pornography under his *nom de plume*. The result meant near financial ruin, for, basing his decision on reputation alone, Lord Chancellor Eldon decreed that Dr Wolcot's copyrights could not be protected under the law. Thus, broken in health, held in ill repute, and impoverished by legal fiat, he retired to the outskirts of London, keeping himself alive with 'fire, flannel, and brandy,' yet still composing an occasional verse with the aid of a charitable amanuensis. In 1812, a good portion of the *Carlton House Fête* was devoted to recapitulating his career as Peter Pindar for the benefit of a new generation raised on Byron, Scott, and Tom Moore. Some few still remembered him, however. William Hazlitt concluded his lectures on the English Comic Writers in January 1819 with a panegyric on his old favourite:

> *The bard in whom the nation and the king delighted, is old and blind, but still merry and wise:— remembering how he has made the world laugh in his time, and not repenting of the mirth he has given . . . tagging a rhyme or conning his own epitaph; and waiting for the last summons, Grateful and Contented!*

But even as Hazlitt spoke these words at the Surrey Institute, Dr John Wolcot was dead in fact.

It is not surprising that Dr Wolcot should have outlived his reputation as Peter Pindar. Peter's subject matter was ephemeral, his verse composed in haste and never revised. Dr Wolcot had no illusions about his work, no compulsion to play latterday Juvenal or Persius, or Horace. Peter Pindar's satires were written to sell. Only when the political tide shifted against him did he have cause to complain, 'Satire is a bad trade'. His earlier popularity, after all, was based on the factors that operated against its enduring. It exploited current fads, fancies, attitudes and issues as well as personalities, none enduring in themselves. What interest remains in the poems relies on the techniques that seemed secondary at the time of composition: the verses seldom suffer from repetition of form, and exploit all kinds—epigrams, parodies, political songs, imitations, inscriptions, fables, epistles, mock-heroic epics, verse essays, and songs after the Greek Anthology. Peter's style is similarly varied and flexible; he could imitate Milton in one stanza, Butler in the next:

With dewy gems adorning herbs and flow'r,
Mov'd meek-eyed Evening on the western hills
With modest mien, and on the calm expanse
Of ocean's mirror look'd, and looking ting'd
Its heaving bosom with a roseate blush;
A blush empyreal!

Now Madam Eve, with gown of pink
Stepp'd down to Neptune's tap to drink,
Where Phoebus just before had been
At his old fam'd salt-water inn.

Peter offered something to all tastes, but his fare was prepared with a facility fatal to enduring fame.

Perhaps it is only due to the law of averages that, of the thousands of poems, some of Peter Pindar's works are still read. His ephemeral subject matter is considered no obstacle and can be as easily ignored as not. Still appealing are the little vignettes in which, with a phrase or two, he caricatures a personality or, with an anecdotal narrative, unwinds an old folk tale in lilting rhyme. The present selection is based on an attempt to show Peter in his merry moods, in caricature and narrative and song, manipulating the language in a way that prompted so adept a technician as Robert Burns to marvel, and then to boast: 'I have the honour to preside over the Scottish verse, as no less a personage than Peter Pindar does over the English.'

NOTE ON THE TEXT

The texts are from *The Works of Peter Pindar*, 5 vols., London 1812. Omissions (indicated by . . .) consist entirely of topical allusions introduced as parenthetical asides, and thus not necessary to the meaning of the poems.

MR PETER PINDAR'S Apology for the Variety of Entertainment in his pretty poetical Oleo, is the first thing I shall present to the Public.

Peter's Apology

Ladies, I keep a Rhyme-shop; mine's a trade;
I sell to old and young, to man and maid:
All customers must be obliged; and no man
Wishes more universally to please.
I'd really crawl upon my knees,
T'oblige; particularly, lovely Woman.

Yet some (the Devil take such virtuous times!)
Fastidious, pick a quarrel with my Rhymes,
And beg I'd only deal in love-sick Sonnet.—
How easy, to bid others cease to feed!
On beauty I can quickly *die* indeed;
But, trust me, can't *live long* upon it.

Permit me, Ladies, now to lay before ye
What lately happen'd; therefore a True Story.

A Story

Walking one afternoon along the Strand,
My wondering eyes did suddenly expand
Upon a pretty leash of Country Lasses.
'Heavens! my dear beauteous Angels, how d'ye do?
Upon my soul I'm monstrous glad to see ye.'—
'Swinge! Peter, we are glad to meet with *you*;
We're just to London come: well, pray how be ye?
'We're just a going, while 'tis dark.
Lord! come, for once be so polite,
And condescend to be our Spark.'—

'With all my heart, my Angels.'—On we walk'd,
And much of London, much of Cornwall, talk'd.
Now did I hug myself to think
How much that glorious Structure would surprise;
How much from its awful Grandeur they would shrink
With open mouths and marv'ling eyes.

As near to Ludgate-Hill we drew,
Saint Paul's just opening on our view;
Behold, my lovely Strangers, one and all,
Gave, all at once, a diabolical Squawl;
As if they had been tumbled on the stones,
And some confounded cart had crush'd their bones.

After well frightening people with their cries,
And sticking to a Ribbon-shop their eyes,
They all rush'd in, with sounds enough to stun,
And, clattering all together, thus begun:
'Swinge! here are Colours then, to please;
Delightful things, I vow to Heaven:
Why, not to see such things as these,
We never should have been forgiven.

'Here, here, are clever things: good Lord!
And, Sister, here, upon my word;
Here, here, look; here are beauties to delight:
Why, how a body's heels might dance
Along from Launceston to Penzance,
Before that one might meet with such a sight!'—

'Come, Ladies, 'twill be dark,' cried I, 'I fear:
Pray let us view St Paul's, it is so near.'—
'Lord! Peter,' cried the Girls, 'don't mind Saint Paul;
Sure you're a most *incurious* soul:
Why, we can see the Church another day;
Don't be afraid; Saint Paul's can't *run away*.'

Reader,
If e'er thy bosom felt a thought *sublime*,
Drop tears of pity with the Man of Rhyme.

PETER administereth sage Advice to mercenary Artists, and telleth a most delectable Story of a Country Bumkin and a Peripatetic Razor-seller.

Forbear, my friends, to sacrifice your fame
To sordid Gain, unless that you are starving:
I own, that Hunger will indulgence claim
For hard Stone Heads and Landscape carving,
In order to make haste to *sell* and *eat*;
For there is certainly a charm in meat:

And in rebellious tones will Stomachs speak,
That have not tasted victuals for a week.

But yet there are a mercenary crew,
Who value Fame no more than an old Shoe,
Provided for their Daubs they get a sale;
Just like a man—but stay, I'll tell the Tale.

A Fellow in a market-town,
Most musical, cried Razors up and down,
And offer'd twelve for eighteen-pence:
Which certainly seem'd wondrous cheap,
And for the money quite a heap;
As every man would buy, with cash and sense.

A country Bumkin the great offer heard;
Poor Hodge, who suffer'd by a thick black Beard
That seem'd a Shoe-brush stuck beneath his nose:
With cheerfulness the eighteen-pence he paid,
And proudly to himself, in whispers, said,
'This rascal stole the Razors, I suppose:

'No matter if the Fellow *be* a knave,
Provided that the Razors *shave*:
It sartinly will be a monstrous Prize.'
So home the Clown, with his good fortune, went
Smiling, in heart and soul content,
And quickly soap'd himself to ears and eyes.

Being well lather'd from a dish or tub,
Hodge now began with grinning pain to grub,
Just like a Hedger cutting Furze:
'Twas a vile Razor!—Then the rest he tried—
All were imposters. 'Ah!' Hodge sigh'd,
'I wish my eighteen-pence within my purse.'

In vain to chase his Beard, and bring the Graces,
He cut, and dug and winced, and stamp'd, and swore;
Brought blood, and danc'd, blasphem'd, and made wry faces,
And curs'd each Razor's body o'er and o'er....

Hodge, in a passion, stretch'd his angry jaws,
Vowing the direst vengeance, with clench'd claws,
On the vile Cheat that sold the goods.
'Razors! a damn'd confounded dog,
Not fit to scrape a Hog.'

Hodge sought the Fellow, found him, and begun:
'Perhaps, Master Razor-rogue, to you 'tis fun
That people flay themselves out of their lives:
You rascal, for an hour have I been grubbing,
With Razors just like Oyster-knives.
Sirrah! I tell you, you're a knave,
To cry up Razors that can't shave.'

'Friend,' quoth the Razor-man, 'I am no knave:
As for the Razors you have bought,
Upon my soul, I never thought
That they would shave.'

'Not think they'd shave!' quoth Hodge with wondering eyes,
And voice not much unlike an Indian yell;
'What were they made for then, you dog?' he cries.—
'Made!' quoth the Fellow with a smile,—'to *sell.*'

PETER still continueth to give great Advice, and to exhibit deep Reflection.—He telleth a Miraculous Story.

There is a knack in doing many a thing,
Which labour cannot to perfection bring:
Therefore, however great in your own eyes,
Pray do not Hints from other folks despise....
Then, if you please,
I'll give you the Two Pilgrims and the Peas.

The Pilgrims and the Peas

A True Story

A brace of Sinners, for no good,
Were order'd to the Virgin Mary's shrine,
Who at Loretto dwelt, in Wax, Stone, Wood,
And in a fair white Wig look'd wondrous fine.

Fifty long miles had those sad Rogues to travel,
With something in their shoes much worse than gravel:
In short, their toes so gentle to amuse,
The Priest had order'd peas into their shoes;

A nostrum famous in old Popish times,
For purifying Souls that stunk of crimes;
    A sort of Apostolic salt,
    Which Popish parsons for its powers exalt,
For keeping Souls of Sinners sweet,
Just as our Kitchen-salt keeps Meat.

The Knaves set off on the same day,
Peas in their shoes, to go and pray;
    But very different was their speed, I wot:
One of the Sinners gallop'd on,
Swift as a Bullet from a gun;
    The other limp'd as if he had been shot.

One saw the Virgin soon; *peccavi* cried;
    Had his Soul white-wash'd all so clever;
Then home again he nimbly hied,
    Made fit with Saints above to live for ever.

In coming back, however, let me say,
He met his Brother-rogue about half-way,
Hobbling, with out-stretch'd bum and bending knees,
Damning the *souls* and *bodies* of the *peas*;
His eyes in tears, his cheeks and brows in sweat,
Deep sympathizing with his groaning feet.

'How now,' the light-toed, white-wash'd Pilgrim broke,
    'You lazy lubber?'—
'Ods curse it,' cried the other, 'tis no joke:
My Feet, once hard as any Rock,
    Are now as soft as Blubber.

'Excuse me, Virgin Mary, that I swear:
As for Loretto, I shall not get there;
No, to the Devil my sinful soul must go,
For damme if I ha'nt lost every toe.

    'But, Brother-sinner, pray explain
How 'tis that *you* are not in pain;
    What Power hath work'd a wonder for *your* toes:
Whilst *I* just like a snail am crawling,
Now swearing, now on Saints devoutly bawling,
    While not a rascal comes to ease my woes?

'How is't that *you* can like a Greyhound go,
Merry as if that nought had happen'd, burn ye?'—
'Why,' cried the other grinning, 'you must know,
That just before I ventured on my journey,
    To walk a little more at ease,
    I took the liberty to boil *my* Peas.'

A Poetical and Congratulatory

Epistle

to

James Boswell, Esq.

on

His Journal of a Tour to the Hebrides with the Celebrated Doctor Johnson

O Boswell, Bozzy, Bruce, whate'er thy name,
Thou mighty Shark for anecdote and fame;
Thou Jackall, leading Lion Johnson forth
To eat Macpherson 'midst his native North;
To frighten grave Professors with his roar,
And shake the Hebrides from shore to shore:
All hail!—At length, ambitious Thane, thy rage
To give one spark to Fame's bespangled page,
Is amply gratified; a thousand eyes
Survey thy books with rapture and surprise.
Loud, of thy Tour, a thousand tongues have spoken,
And wondered that thy bones were never broken.

Triumphant, thou through Time's vast gulf shalt sail,
The Pilot of our Literary Whale;
Close to the Classic Rambler shalt thou cling,
Close as a supple Courtier to a King:
Fate shall not shake thee off, with all its power;
Stuck, like a Bat to some old ivied Tower.
Nay, though thy Johnson ne'er had bless'd thy eyes,
Paoli's deeds had raised thee to the skies:
Yes; his broad wing had raised thee (no bad hack),
A Tom-Tit twittering on an Eagle's back.

Thou, curious Scrapmonger, shalt live in song
When Death has still'd the rattle of thy tongue;
E'en future babes to lisp thy name shall learn,
And Bozzy join with Wood and Tommy Hearn,
Who drove the Spiders from much prose and rhyme,
And snatch'd old stories from the jaws of Time.
Sweet is thy page, I ween, that doth recite
How thou and Johnson, arm in arm, one night,
March'd through fair Edinburgh's Pactolian show'rs,
Which Cloacina bountifully pours;

Those gracious show'rs that fraught with fragrance flow,
And *gild*, like Gingerbread, the World below.
How sweetly grumbled too was Sam's remark,
'I smell you, Master Bozzy, in the dark!'
Alas! Historians are confounded dull,
A dim Boeotia reigns in every scull:
Mere Beasts of Burden, broken-winded, slow,
Heavy as Cart-horses, along they go;
While thou, a Will-o-the'-wisp, art here, art there,
Wild darting coruscations every where.

What tasteless mouth can gape, what eye can close,
What head can nod, o'er thy enlivening Prose?
To others' Works, the Works of thy inditing
Are downright Diamonds to the Eyes of Whiting.
Think not I flatter thee, my flippant friend;
For well I know that Flattery would offend:
Yet honest Praise, I'm sure, thou wouldst not shun,
Born with a stomach to digest a tun.
Who can refuse a smile, that reads thy page
Where surly Sam, inflamed with Tory rage,
Nassau *bescoundrels*; and, with anger big,
Swears Whigs are Rogues, and every Rogue a Whig?
Who will not too thy pen's minutiae bless,
That gives Posterity the Rambler's Dress?
Methinks I view his full plain suit of brown,
The large grey bushy wig that graced his crown,
Black worsted stockings, little silver buckles,
And shirt that had no ruffles for his knuckles.
I mark the brown great-coat of cloth he wore,
That two huge Patagonian pockets bore,
Which Patagonians (wondrous to unfold!)
Would fairly both his Dictionaries hold.
I see the Rambler on a large bay Mare,
Just like a Centaur, every danger dare;
On a full gallop dash the yielding wind,
The Colt and Bozzy scampering close behind.

Of Lady Lochbuy with what glee we read,
Who offered Sam, for breakfast, cold Sheep's Head;
Who, press'd and worried by this Dame so civil,
Wish'd the *sheep's* head and *woman's* at the Devil!

I see you sailing both in Buchan's Pot:
Now storming an old woman and her cot;
Who, terrified at each tremendous Shape,
Deemed you two Demons ready for a rape.
I see all marvelling at Macleod's together,
At Sam's remarks on whey and tanning leather.
At Corrichatachin's, the Lord knows how,
I see thee, Bozzy, drunk as David's Sow,
And begging, with raised eyes and lengthen'd chin,
Heaven not to damn thee for the deadly sin.
I see too the stern Moralist regale,
And pen a Latin Ode to Mistress Thrale.
I see, without a night-cap on his head,
Rare sight! bald Sam in the Pretender's bed.
I hear (what's wonderful), unsought by studying,
His classic Dissertation upon Pudding:
Of Provost Jopp I mark the marvelling face,
Who gave the Rambler's freedom with a grace.
I see too, travelling from the Isle of Egg,
The humble servant of a horse's leg;
And Snip the Taylor, from the Isle of Muck,
Who stitch'd in Sky with tolerable luck.
I see the Horn that Drunkards must adore;
The Horn, the mighty Horn, of Rorie More;
And bloody Shields that guarded Hearts in quarrels,
Now guard from Rats the milk and butter Barrels.
Methinks the Caledonian Dame I see
Familiar sitting on the Rambler's knee;
Charming, with kisses sweet, the chuckling Sage;
Melting with sweetest smiles the frost of age;
Like Sol, who darts at times a cheerful ray
O'er the wan visage of a Winter's Day.
'Do it again, my dear,' I hear Sam cry:
'See who first tires, my Charmer, you or I.'
I see thee stuffing, with a hand uncouth,
An old dried Whiting in thy Johnson's mouth;
And lo! I see, with all his might and main,
Thy Johnson spit the Whiting out again.
Rare Anecdotes! 'tis Anecdotes like these
That bring thee glory, and the Million please:
On these shall future times delighted stare,
Thou charming Haberdasher of Small Ware.

Stewart and Robertson from thee shall learn,
The *simple* charms of History to discern:
To thee, fair History's palm shall Livy yield,
And Tacitus to Bozzy leave the field:
Joe Miller's self, whose page such Fun provokes,
Shall quit his shroud, to grin at Bozzy's Jokes.
How are we all with rapture touched, to see
Where, when, and at what hour, you swallowed Tea;
How once, to grace this Asiatic treat,
Came Haddocks, which the Rambler could not eat!

Pleased, on thy Book thy Sovereign's eye-balls roll,
Who loves a Gossip's Story from his soul.
Blest with the memory of the Persian king,
He every body knows, and every thing;
Who's dead, who's married, what poor Girl beguil'd
Hath lost a paramour and found a child;
Which Gardener hath most cabbages and peas,
And which Old Woman hath most hives of bees;
Which Farmer boasts the most prolific sows,
Cocks, hens, geese, turkeys, goats, sheep, bulls, and cows;
Which Barber best the Ladies' locks can curl;
Which house in Windsor sells the finest Purl;
Which Chimney-sweep best beats, in gold array,
His brush and shovel, on the first of May;
Whose Dancing-dogs in rigadoons excel;
And whose the Puppet-show that bears the bell;
Which clever smith the prettiest Man-trap makes,
To save from thieves the Royal ducks and drakes,
The Guinea hens and peacocks, with their eggs,
And catch his loving subjects by the legs.
Oh! since the Prince of Gossips reads thy book,
To what high honours may not Bozzy look?
The sunshine of *his* Smile may soon be thine:
Perchance, in Converse thou mayst hear him shine:
Perchance, to stamp thy merit through the Nation,
He begs of Johnson's Life thy Dedication;
Asks questions of thee, O thou lucky elf,
And *kindly* answers every one himself.
Blest with the classic learning of a College,
Our King is *not* a miser in his *knowledge*:
Nought in the storehouse of his brains turns musty;

No Razor-wit, for want of use, grows rusty:
Whate'er his head suggests, whate'er he knows,
Free as Election Beer from tubs it flows;
Yet, ah! superior far, it boasts the merit
Of never fuddling people with the spirit.

Say, Bozzy, when, to bless our anxious sight,
When shall thy Volume burst the gates of light?
Oh! clothed in calf, ambitious Brat, be born;
Our kitchens, parlours, libraries, adorn.
My Fancy's keen anticipating eye,
A thousand charming Anecdotes can spy: . . .
Of George, whose Brain, if right the mark I hit,
Forms one huge Cyclopedia of wit;
That holds the wisdom of a thousand ages,
And *frightens* all his Workmen and his Pages.
O Bozzy, still thy tell-tale plan pursue:
The World is wondrous fond of something new;
And let but Scandal's breath embalm the page,
It lives a welcome guest from age to age.
Not only say who breathes an arrant knave,
But who hath sneak'd a rascal to his grave:
Make o'er his turf (in Virtue's cause) a rout,
And, like a damned good Christian, pull him out.
Without a fear, on families harangue;
Say who shall lose their ears, and who shall hang;
Publish the demireps, and punks; nay more,
Declare what virtuous wife shall be a whore.
Thy brilliant brain *conjecture* can supply,
To charm through every leaf the eager eye.
The Blue Stocking society describe,
And give thy comment on each joke and jibe:
Tell what the Women are, their wit, their quality,
And dip them in thy streams of immortality.

Let Lord Macdonald threat thy breech to kick,
And o'er thy shrinking shoulders shake his stick:
Treat with contempt the menace of this Lord;
'Tis History's province, Bozzy, to *record.*
Though Wilkes abuse thy Brain, that airy Mill,
And swear poor Johnson murdered by thy quill;
What's that to thee? Why, let the Victim bleed;

Thy end is answered, if the Nation *read.*
The fiddling Knight, and tuneful Mistress Thrale,
Who frequent hobb'd or nobb'd with Sam in ale,
Snatch up the pen (as thirst of fame inspires),
To write his jokes and stories by their fires;
Then why not thou each joke and tale enrol,
Who, like a watchful Cat before a hole,
Full twenty years (inflamed with letter'd pride)
Didst mousing sit before Sam's mouth so wide,
To catch as many scraps as thou wert able,
A very Lazarus at the Rich Man's table?
What though against thee Porters bounce the door,
And bid thee hunt for secrets there no more;
With pen and ink so ready at thy coat,
Exciseman-like, each syllable to note,
That, given to Printer's Devils (a precious load!),
On wings of print comes flying all abroad?
Watch then the venal Valets, smack the Maids,
And try with gold to make them rogues and jades.
Yet should their honesty thy bribes resent;
Fly to thy fertile genius, and *invent*:
Like old Voltaire, who placed his greatest glory
In cooking up an entertaining story;
Who laughed at Truth, whene'er her simple tongue
Would snatch Amusement from a tale or song.

Oh! while amid the Anecdotic mine
Thou labour'st hard to bid thy Hero shine,
Run to Bolt Court, exert thy Curll-like soul,
And fish for *golden* leaves from hole to hole:
Find when he ate and drank, and cough'd and sneezed;
Let all his *motions* in thy Book be squeezed:
On tales, however strange, impose thy claw;
Yes, let thy Amber lick up every Straw:
Sam's nods, and winks, and laughs, will form a treat;
For *all* that *breathes* of Johnson *must* be *great.*

Blest be thy labours, most adventurous Bozzy,
Bold rival of Sir John and Dame Piozzi;
Heavens, with what Laurels shall thy head be crown'd!
A Grove, a Forest, shall thy ears surround.
Yes: while the Rambler shall a Comet blaze,
And gild a world of darkness with its rays,

Thee too that world with wonderment shall hail,
A lively *bouncing* Cracker at his tail.

POSTSCRIPT

As Mr Boswell's Journal hath afforded such universal pleasure by the relation of minute incidents, and the Great Moralist's opinions of men and things, during his Northern Tour; it will be adding greatly to the Anecdotal treasury, as well as making Mr Boswell happy, to communicate part of a Dialogue that took place between Dr Johnson, and the Author of this Congratulatory Epistle, a few months before the Doctor paid the great debt of nature. The Doctor was very cheerful that day: had on a black coat and waistcoat, a black plush pair of breeches, and black worsted stockings; a handsome grey wig, a shirt, a muslin neckcloth, a black pair of buttons in his shirt-sleeves, a pair of shoes ornamented with the very identical little buckles that accompanied the Philosopher to the Hebrides; his nails were very neatly pared, and his beard fresh-shaved with a razor fabricated by the ingenious Mr Savigny.

P.P. 'Pray Doctor, what is your opinion of Mr Boswell's literary powers?'

Johnson. 'Sir, my opinion is, that whenever Bozzy expires, he will create no vacuum in the region of literature: he seems strongly affected by the *cacoethes scribendi*; wishes to be thought a *rara avis*, and in truth so he is—your knowledge in Ornithology, Sir, will easily discover to what species of bird I allude.'

(Here the Doctor shook his head, and laughed.)

P.P. 'What think you, Sir, of his Account of Corsica?—of his character of Paoli?'

Johnson. 'Sir, he hath made a Mountain of a Wart. But Paoli *has* virtues. The Account is a farrago of disgusting egotism and pompous inanity.'

P.P. 'I have heard it whispered, Doctor, that should you die before him, Mr Boswell means to write your Life.'

Johnson. 'Sir, he cannot mean me so irreparable an injury. Which of us shall die first, is only known to the Great Disposer of events; but were I sure that James Boswell would write *my* Life, I do not know whether I would not anticipate the measure by taking *his*.'

(Here he made three or four strides across the room, and returned to his chair with violent emotion.)

P.P. 'I am afraid that he means to do you the favour.'

Johnson. 'He dares not: he would make a Scarecrow of me. I give him liberty to fire his blunderbuss in his own face, but not murder *me*. Sir, I heed not *his* [self-puffing]. Boswell write my Life! why the fellow possesses not abilities for writing the Life of an *ephemeron*.'

Bozzy and Piozzi

or the

British Biographers

A Town Eclogue

The Argument

On the Death of Dr Johnson, a Number of People, ambitious of being distinguished from the mute Part of their Species, set about relating and printing Stories and Bon-mots of that celebrated Moralist. Among the most zealous, though not the most enlightened, appeared Mr Boswell and Madame Piozzi, the Hero and Heroine of our Eclogue. They are supposed to have in Contemplation the Life of Johnson; and, to prove their biographical Abilities, appeal to Sir John Hawkins for his Decision on their respective Merits, by Quotations from their printed Anecdotes of the Doctor. Sir John hears them with uncommon Patience, and determines very properly on the Pretensions of the contending Parties.

When Johnson sought (as Shakespeare says) that bourn
From whence, alas! no travellers return
(In humbler English, when the Doctor died),
Apollo whimper'd, and the Muses cried;
Parnassus moped for days, in business slack,
And, like a Hearse, the Hill was hung with black;
Minerva, sighing for her favourite Son,
Pronounced, with lengthen'd face, the World undone;
Her Owl too hooted in so loud a style,
That people might have heard the Bird a mile:
Jove wiped his eyes so red; and told his Wife,
He ne'er made Johnson's equal in his life;
And that 'twould be a long time ere, if ever,
His art could form a fellow half so clever:
Venus, of all the little Loves the Dam,
With all the Graces, sobb'd for Brother Sam;
Such were the heavenly howlings for his death,
As if Dame Nature had resigned her breath.
Nor less sonorous was the grief, I ween,
Amidst the natives of our earthly scene:
From Beggars, to the Great who hold the helm,
One Johnso-mania raged through all the Realm.

'Who,' cried the World, 'can match his Prose or Rhyme?
O'er Wits of modern days he towers sublime:

An Oak, wide-spreading o'er the Shrubs below,
That round his roots, with puny foliage, blow;
A Pyramid amidst some barren waste,
That frowns o'er Huts the sport of every blast;
A mighty Atlas, whose aspiring head
O'er distant regions cast an awful shade.
By Kings and Beggars, lo! his tales are told,
And every Sentence glows a Grain of Gold.
Blest who his philosophic Phiz can take,
Catch even his weaknesses, his Noddle's shake,
The lengthen'd Lip of scorn, the forehead's Scowl,
The louring Eye's contempt, and Bear-like Growl.
In vain the Critics aim their toothless rage;
Mere Sprats, that venture war with Whales to wage:
Unmoved he stands, and feels their force no more
Than some huge Rock amidst the watry roar,
That calmly bears the tumults of the deep,
And howling tempests that as well may sleep.'

Strong 'midst the Rambler's Cronies was the rage
To fill with Sam's Bon-mots and Tales the page;
Mere Flies, that buzz'd around his setting Ray,
And bore a splendour on their wings away:
Thus round his orb the pigmy Planets run,
And catch their little lustre from the Sun.

At length, rush'd forth two Candidates for fame;
A Scotchman one, and one a London Dame:
That, by th'emphatic Johnson christened Bozzy;
This, by the Bishop's licence, Dame Piozzi;
Whose widowed name, by Topers loved, was Thrale,
Bright in the annals of Election Ale....
Each seized with ardour wild the grey-goose Quill:
Each set to work the intellectual Mill;
That Pecks of Bran so coarse began to pour,
To one poor solitary Grain of Flour.

Forth rush'd to light their Books; but who should say,
Which bore the palm of Anecdote away?
This to decide, the rival Wits agreed
Before Sir John their tales and jokes to read;
And let the Knight's opinion in the strife,
Declare the properest pen to write Sam's Life:

Sir John, renowned for Musical palavers;
The Prince, the King, the Emperor, of Quavers:
Sharp in solfeggi, as the sharpest Needle;
Great in the noble art of tweedle-tweedle;
Of Music's College formed to be a Fellow,
Fit for *Mus. D.* or *Maestro di Capella*;
Whose Volume, though it here and there offends,
Boasts German merit—makes by *bulk* amends.
High-placed the venerable Quarto sits,
Superior frowning o'er Octavo wits
And Duodecimos: ignoble scum,
Poor prostitutes to every vulgar thumb;
While, undefiled by literary rage,
He bears a spotless leaf from age to age.

Like School-boys, lo! before a two-armed chair
That held the Knight wise-judging, stood the Pair:
Or like two Ponies on the sporting ground,
Prepared to gallop when the drum should sound,
The Couple ranged; for victory both as keen,
As for a tottering Bishopric a Dean;
Or patriot Burke, for giving glorious bastings
To that intolerable fellow Hastings.
Thus with their songs contended Virgil's Swains,
And made the valleys vocal with their strains,
Before some Greybeard sage, whose judgement ripe
Gave Goats for Prizes to the prettiest pipe.

'Alternately in Anecdotes go on;
But first begin you, Madam,' cried Sir John.
The thankful Dame low curtseyed to the Chair,
And thus, for victory panting, read the Fair:—

MADAME PIOZZI

Sam Johnson was of Michael Johnson born;
Whose shop of books did Litchfield town adorn:
Wrong-headed, stubborn as a halter'd Ram;
In short, the model of our Hero Sam:
Inclined to madness too; for when his shop
Fell down, for want of cash to buy a prop,
For fear the thieves might steal the vanish'd store
He duly went each night and lock'd the door.

BOZZY

While Johnson was in Edinburgh, my Wife
To please his palate, studied for her life:
With every rarity she fill'd her house,
And gave the Doctor, for his dinner, grouse.

MADAME PIOZZI

Dear Doctor Johnson was in size an Ox;
And from his uncle Andrew learn'd to box:
A man to Wrestlers and to Bruisers dear,
Who kept the ring in Smithfield a whole year.
The Doctor had an uncle too, ador'd
By jumping gentry, called Cornelius Ford;
Who jump'd in Boots, which Jumpers never choose,
Far as a famous Jumper jump'd in Shoes.

BOZZY

At supper rose a dialogue on Witches,
When Crosbie said there could not be such bitches;
And that 'twas blasphemy to think such Hags
Could stir up storms, and on their broomstick Nags
Gallop along the air with wondrous pace,
And boldly fly in God Almighty's face:
But Johnson answer'd him, 'There *might* be Witches;
Nought proved the non-existence of the bitches.'

MADAME PIOZZI

When Thrale, as nimble as a Boy at School,
Leap'd, though fatigued with hunting, o'er a Stool;
The Doctor, proud the same grand feat to do,
His powers exerted, and jump'd over too;
And, though he might a broken back bewail,
He scorn'd to be eclips'd by Mister Thrale.

BOZZY

At Ulinish, our Friend, to pass the time,
Regaled us with his Knowledges sublime;
Showed that all sorts of Learning fill'd his knob,
And that in Butchery he could bear a bob.
He sagely told us of the different feat
Employed to kill the Animals we eat.
'An Ox,' says he, 'in country and in town,
Is by the Butchers constantly knock'd down;
As for that lesser animal, a Calf,
The knock is really not so strong by half;

The beast is only stunn'd; but as for Goats,
And Sheep, and Lambs, the Butchers cut their throats.
Those fellows only want to keep them quiet,
Not choosing that the brutes should breed a riot.'

MADAME PIOZZI

When Johnson was a child, and swallowed pap,
'Twas in his Mother's old maid Catherine's lap.
There while he sat, he took in wondrous Learning;
For much his bowels were for Knowledge yearning:
There heard the story we Britons brag on,
The story of Saint George and eke the Dragon.

BOZZY

When Foote his leg, by some misfortune, broke,
Says *I* to Johnson, all by way of joke,
'Sam, Sir, in Paragraph will soon be clever,
And take off Peter better now than ever.'
On which says Johnson, without hesitation,
'George will rejoice at Foote's *depeditation.*'
On which says *I* (a penetrating elf!),
'Doctor, I'm sure you coin'd that word yourself.'
On which he laugh'd, and said I had divin'd it,
For *bonâ fide* he had really coin'd it:
'And yet, of all the words I've coin'd,' says he,
'My Dictionary, Sir, contains but three.'

MADAME PIOZZI

The Doctor said, 'In literary matters
A Frenchman goes not deep; he only smatters;'
Then ask'd what could be hoped for from the dogs;
Fellows that lived eternally on Frogs.

BOZZY

In grave procession to St Leonard's College,
Well stuffed with every sort of useful knowledge,
We stately walk'd, as soon as supper ended:
The Landlord and the Waiter both attended.
The Landlord, skill'd a piece of grease to handle,
Before us march'd, and held a tallow Candle;
A Lantern (some famed Scotchman its creator)
With equal grace was carried by the Waiter.
Next morning, from our beds we took a leap,
And found ourselves much better for our sleep.

MADAME PIOZZI

In Lincolnshire, a Lady showed our Friend
A Grotto, that she wish'd him to commend.
Quoth she, 'How *cool* in summer this abode!'—
'Yes, Madam,' answer'd Johnson; 'for a *toad*.'

BOZZY

Between old Scalpa's rugged isle and Rasay's,
The wind was vastly boisterous in our faces:
'Twas glorious, Johnson's figure to set sight on;
High in the boat, he looked a noble Triton.
But, lo! to damp our pleasure Fate concurs,
For Joe (the blockhead!) lost his Master's spurs:
This for the Rambler's temper was a rubber,
Who wonder'd Joseph could be such a lubber.

MADAME PIOZZI

I ask'd him if he knock'd Tom Osborne down;
As such a tale was current through the town.
Says I, 'Do tell me, Doctor, what befell.'—
'Why, dearest Lady, there is nought to tell:
I ponder'd on the properest mode to treat him;
The dog was impudent, and so I beat him.
Tom, like a fool, proclaim'd his fancied wrongs;
Others that I belaboured, held their tongues.'

Did any one, 'that he was happy,' cry;
Johnson would tell him plumply, 'twas a lie.
A Lady told him she was really so;
On which he sternly answer'd, 'Madam, no.
Sickly you are, and ugly; foolish, poor;
And therefore can't be *happy*, I am sure.
'Twould make a fellow hang himself, whose ear
Were, from *such creatures*, forced such stuff to hear.'

BOZZY

Lo! when we landed on the Isle of Mull,
The megrims got into the Doctor's scull;
With such bad humours he began to fill,
I thought he would not go to Icolmkill:
But, lo! those megrims (wonderful to utter!)
Were banish'd all by tea, and bread and butter....

I said, I liked not Goose, and mention'd why:
'One smells it roasting on the spit,' quoth I.—
'*You*, Madam,' cried the Doctor with a frown,
'Are always gorging, stuffing something down:
Madam, 'tis very natural to suppose,
If in the pantry you will poke your nose,
Your maw with every sort of victuals swelling,
That you *must* want the bliss of dinner-smelling.'

BOZZY

As at Argyle's grand house my hat I took,
To seek my alehouse, thus began the Duke:
'Pray, Mister Boswell, won't you have some tea?'
To this I made my bow, and did agree.
Then to the drawing-room we both retreated,
Where Lady Betty Hamilton was seated
Close by the Duchess; who, in deep discourse,
Took no more notice of *me* than a Horse.—
Next day, *myself* and Doctor Johnson took
Our hats, to go and wait upon the Duke.
Next to himself the Duke did Johnson place;
But I, thank God, sat *second* to his Grace.
The place was due most surely to my merits;
And, faith, I was in very pretty spirits.
I plainly saw (my penetration such is),
I was not yet in favour with the Duchess.
Thought I, 'I am not disconcerted yet;
Before we part, I'll give her Grace a *sweat*.'
Then looks of intrepidity I put on,
And ask'd her if she'd have a plate of mutton.
This was a glorious deed, must be confess'd;
I knew I was the *Duke's* and not *her* guest.
Knowing (as I'm a man of tip-top breeding)
That *great folks* drink no healths while they are feeding;
I took my glass, and, looking at her Grace,
I stared her like a Devil in the face;
And in respectful terms, as was my duty,
Said I, 'My Lady Duchess, I salute ye.'
Most audible indeed was my salute,
For which some folks will say I was a Brute:
But faith, it dash'd her, as I knew it would;
But then, I knew that I was flesh and blood.

MADAME PIOZZI

Once at our house, amidst our Attic feasts,
We liken'd our Acquaintances to Beasts;
As for example—some to calves and hogs,
And some to bears and monkeys, cats and dogs.
We said (which charm'd the Doctor much, no doubt),
His Mind was like of Elephants the Snout,
That could pick pins up, yet possess'd the vigour
For trimming well the jacket of a Tiger.

BOZZY

August the fifteenth, Sunday, Mister Scott
Did breakfast with us: when upon the spot,
To him, and unto Doctor Johnson, lo!
Sir William Forbes, so clever, did I show;
A man that doth not after roguery hanker;
A charming Christian, *though* by trade a Banker;
Made too of good companionable stuff,
And this, I think, is saying full enough.
And yet it is but justice to record,
That when he had the Measles, 'pon my word,
The people seemed in such a dreadful fright,
His house was all surrounded day and night,
As if they apprehended some great evil;
A General Conflagration, or the Devil.
And when he better'd, oh! 'twas grand to see 'em
Like mad folks dance, and hear 'em sing *Te Deum.*

MADAME PIOZZI

Quoth Johnson, "Who d'ye think my Life will write?"
'Goldsmith,' said I. Quoth he, 'The dog's vile Spite,
Besides the fellow's monstrous love of Lying,
Would doubtless make the Book not worth the buying.'

BOZZY

That worthy gentleman, good Mister Scott,
Said, 'twas our Socrates's luckless lot
To have the Waiter, a sad nasty blade,
To make, poor Gentleman! his Lemonade;
Which Waiter, much against the Doctor's wish,
Put with his *paws* the sugar in the dish.
The Doctor, vexed at such a filthy fellow,
Began, with great propriety, to bellow;
Then up he took the dish, and nobly flung

The liquor out of window on the dung:
And Doctor Scott declared, that, by his frown,
He thought he would have knock'd the fellow down.

MADAME PIOZZI

Dear Doctor Johnson left off Drinks fermented;
With quarts of chocolate and cream contented:
Yet often down his throat's prodigious gutter.
Poor man! he poured a flood of melted butter.

BOZZY

With glee the Doctor did my Girl behold;
Her name Veronica, just four months old.
This name Veronica, a name though quaint,
Belonged originally to a Saint:
But to my old Great-grandam it was given,
As fine a woman as e'er went to Heaven;
And, what must add to her importance much,
This Lady's genealogy was Dutch.
The Man who did espouse this Dame divine,
Was Alexander, Earl of Kincardine;
Who poured along my Body, like a Sluice,
The noble, noble, noble blood of Bruce:
And who that own'd this blood could well refuse
To make the World acquainted with the *news*?
But to return unto my charming Child:
About our Doctor Johnson she was wild;
And when he left off speaking, she would flutter,
Squawl for him to begin again, and sputter;
And to be near him a strong wish express'd:
Which proves he was not *such* a horrid Beast.
Her fondness for the Doctor pleased me greatly;
On which I loud exclaimed in language stately,
Nay, if I recollect aright, I *swore*,
I'd to her fortune add five hundred more.

MADAME PIOZZI

One day, as we were all in talking lost,
My Mother's favourite Spaniel stole the toast;
On which immediately I screamed, 'Fie on her.'
'Fie, Belle,' said I, 'you used to be on honour.'—
'Yes,' Johnson cried; 'but, Madam, pray be told,
The reason for the vice is, Belle grows *old*.'
But Johnson never could the Dog abide,

Because my Mother wash'd and comb'd his hide.
The truth on't is, Belle was not too well bred,
But always would *insist* on being fed;
And very often too, the saucy Slut
Insisted upon having the *first cut.*

BOZZY

Last night much care for Johnson's Cold was used,
Who hitherto without his nightcap *snooz'd.*
That nought might treat so wonderful a man ill,
Sweet Miss MacLeod did make a Cap of Flannel;
And, after putting it about his head,
She gave him Brandy as he went to bed.

MADAME PIOZZI

One night we parted at the Doctor's door,
When thus I said, as I had said before:
'Don't forget Dicky, Doctor; mind poor Dick.'
On which he turn'd round on his heel so quick;
'Madam,' quoth he, 'and when I've served *that* elf,
I guess I then may go and hang myself.'

BOZZY

At night, well soak'd with rain, and wondrous weary,
We got as wet as Shags to Inverary.
We supp'd most royally; were vastly frisky;
When Johnson order'd up a gill of Whisky.
Taking the glass, says I, 'Here's Mistress Thrale.'—
'Drink her in Whisky not,' said he, 'but Ale.'

MADAME PIOZZI

The Doctor had a Cat, and christen'd Hodge,
That at his house in Fleet-street used to lodge.
This Hodge grew old, and sick; and used to wish
That all his dinners might be form'd of Fish.
To please poor Hodge, the Doctor, all so kind,
Went out, and bought him Oysters to his mind.
This every day he did; nor ask'd Black Frank,
Who deemed himself of much too high a rank,
With vulgar fish-fags to be forced to chat,
And purchase Oysters for a mangy Cat.

SIR JOHN

For God's sake stay each Anecdotic scrap;
Let me draw breath, and take a trifling nap.

With one half-hour's restoring slumber blest,
And Heaven's assistance, I may *bear* the *rest.*
Aside.]—What have I done, inform me, gracious Lord,
That thus my ears with nonsense should be bored?
Oh! if I do not in the trial die,
The Devil and all his Brimstone I defy:
No punishment in *other* worlds I fear;
My crimes will all be expiated *here.*
Ah! ten times happier was my lot of yore,
When, raised to *consequence* that all adore,
I sat each session, King-like, in the Chair,
Awed every rank, and made the Million stare;
Lord-paramount o'er every Justice riding,
In causes, with a Turkish sway, deciding.
Yes, like a noble Bashaw of three tails,
I spread a fear and trembling through the Jails
Blest, have I brow-beaten each thief and strumpet,
And blasted on them, like the last day's Trumpet.
I know no paltry weakness of the soul;
No snivelling pity dares my deeds control:
Ashamed, the weakness of my King I hear;
Who, childish, drops on every death a tear.
Return, return again, thou glorious hour
That to my grasp once gavest my idol, Power;
When at my feet the humble knaves would fall,
The thundering Jupiter of Hick's Hall.—
The Knight thus finishing his speech, so fair,
Sleep pulled him gently backward in his chair;
Oped wide the mouth that oft on Jail-birds swore,
Then raised his nasal organ to a roar
That actually surpassed in tone and grace
The grumbled ditties of his favourite Bass.

Sir Joshua Reynolds

Is it not astonishing that the Life of so great a man as Sir Joshua Reynolds should not have been written? a Painter who possessed more of the charming Art than almost any single professor that ever existed. But Fame proclaimeth Mister James Boswell to be *big* with the Biography of this celebrated Artist, and ready to sink into the straw.

See Johnson's angry Ghost, ye Gods, arise!
He drops his nether lip, and rolls his eyes;
And roars, 'O Bozzy, Bozzy, spare the dead!
Raise not thy biographic guillotine;
Decapitate no more with that machine,
Nor frighten Horror with a second head:—
From Reynold's neck the ponderous weapon keep:
Cease, *Anthropophagus*, to murder sleep.'

There is a wonderful energy, as well as sonorous sublimity, in this polysyllabic expression of the Ghost of our immortal Moralist and Lexicographer, not obvious to the *minora sidera* of Literature. The word *anthropophagus* is a derivative from the Greek, signifying *man-eater*; and Mister James Boswell having regaled most plentifully on the Carcase of Doctor Johnson, and meaning to make as hearty a meal on the Body of Sir Joshua Reynolds, furnisheth the perturbed Spectre with an appellative of fortunate propriety.

Johnson and Reynolds, lo, for ever lost!
Of no *great man* has Bozzy now to boast;
Of no *rich table* now can Bozzy brag:
Indeed, like faded Beauties, he will say,
'Envy must own I've had my shining day.'—
What wert thou?—an illuminated rag!
But what's become of boastful Bozzy now?
Deep sunk in mournful solitude art thou.
Amidst thy small tin-box, so drear and dark,
No courted Genius casts a lucky spark:
Nothing to gild thy solitary tinder,
Save the rude flint and steel of Peter Pindar.

Ode IX to the Royal Academicians

The gossiping PETER telleth a strange Story; and true, though strange-Seemeth to entertain no very elevated Opinions of the Wisdom of Kings—Hinteth at the narrow Escape of Sir Joshua Reynolds—Mr Ramsay's Riches.—A Recommendation of Flattery, as a Specific in Fortune-making.

I'm told, and I believe the story,
  That a fam'd Queen of Northern brutes,
A Gentlewoman of prodigious glory,
  Whom every sort of epithet well suits;
Whose husband dear, just happening to provoke her,
Was shoved to Heaven upon a red-hot poker;
Sent to a certain King, not King of France,
  Desiring by Sir Joshua's hand his Phiz.—
  What did the Royal Quiz?
Why, damn'd genteely, sat to Mister Dance!
Then sent it to the Northern Queen,
As sweet a bit of *wood* as e'er was seen;
And therefore most unlike the princely Head;
He might as well have sent a pig of lead.

Down every throat the piece was cramm'd
As done by Reynolds, and deservedly damn'd;
  For as to Master Dance's Art,
  It ne'er was worth a single——.
Reader, I blush; am delicate this time:
So let thy impudence supply the rhyme.

  Thank God that Monarchs cannot Taste control,
  And make each Subject's poor submissive soul
Admire the work that judgement oft cries fie on:
  Had things been so, poor Reynolds we had seen
  Painting a Barber's Pole, an Ale-house Queen,
The *Cat and Gridiron*, or the *Old Red Lion*:
At Plympton perhaps, for some grave Doctor Slop,
Painting the pots and bottles of the shop;
Or in the Drama, to get meat to munch,
His brush divine had pictured scenes for Punch:
Whilst West was whelping, 'midst his paints,
Moses and Aaron, and all sorts of Saints;
Adams and Eves, and Snakes and Apples,
And Devils for beautifying certain Chapels.

But Reynolds is no favourite, that's the matter;
He has not learnt the noble art, to flatter.

Thrice-happy times, when Monarchs find them hard things,
To teach us what to view with admiration;
And, like their heads on halfpence and brass farthings,
Make their opinions current through the nation!

I've heard that Ramsay, when he died,
Left just nine rooms well stuff'd with Queens and Kings;
From whence all nations might have been supplied,
That long'd for valuable things.
Viceroys, Ambassadors, and Plenipos,
Bought them to join their raree-shows
In foreign parts,
And show the progress of the British Arts.

Whether they purchas'd by the pound or yard,
I cannot tell, because I never heard;
But this I know, his shop was like a fair,
And dealt most largely in this Royal ware.
See what it is to gain a Monarch's smile;—
And hast thou miss'd it, Reynolds, all this while?
How stupid! prithee, seek the Courtier's school,
And learn to manufacture oil of fool.

Flattery's the turnpike-road to Fortune's door:
Truth is a narrow lane, all full of quags,
Leading to broken heads, abuse, and rags,
And workhouses, sad refuge for the poor!

Flattery's a Mountebank so spruce, gets riches;
Truth, a plain Simon Pure, a Quaker preacher,
A moral-mender, a disgusting teacher,
That never got a sixpence by her speeches.

PETER challengeth Courtiers to equal his Intrepidity, and proveth his Superiority of Courage by giving a delectable Tale of Dumplings.

What modern Courtier, pray, hath got the face
To say to Majesty, 'O King!
At *such* a time, in *such* a place,
You did a very foolish thing?'

What Courtier, not a foe to his own glory,
Would publish of his King this simple Story?—

The Apple-dumplings and a King

Once on a time, a Monarch, tired with whooping,
Whipping and spurring,
Happy in worrying
A poor, defenceless, harmless Buck
(The Horse and Rider wet as muck),
From his high consequence and wisdom stooping,
Enter'd, through curiosity, a cot
Where sat a poor Old Woman and her pot.

The wrinkled, blear-eyed, good old Granny,
In this same cot, illumed by many a cranny,
Had finish'd Apple-dumplings for her pot:
In tempting row the naked Dumplings lay,
When, lo! the Monarch, in his usual way,
Like Lightning spoke: 'What's this? what's this? what? what?'

Then, taking up a Dumpling in his hand,
His eyes with admiration did expand,
And oft did Majesty the Dumpling grapple:
' 'Tis monstrous, monstrous hard indeed,' he cried:
'What makes it, pray, so hard?'—The Dame replied,
Low curtseying, 'Please your Majesty, the Apple.'—

'Very astonishing indeed! strange thing!'
(Turning the Dumpling round, rejoined the King).
' 'Tis most extraordinary then, all this is;
It beats Pinetti's conjuring all to pieces:
Strange I should never of a Dumpling dream!
But, Goody, tell me where, where, where's the Seam?'

'Sir, there's no Seam,' quoth she; 'I never knew
That folks did Apple-dumplings *sew*.'—
'No!' cried the staring Monarch with a grin:
'How, how the devil got the Apple in?'

On which the Dame the curious scheme revealed
By which the Apple lay so sly concealed;
Which made the Solomon of Britain start:

Who to the Palace with full speed repaired,
And Queen and Princesses so beauteous scared,
    All with the wonders of the Dumpling Art.
There did he labour one whole week, to show
    The wisdom of an Apple-dumpling Maker;
And, lo! so deep was Majesty in dough,
    The Palace seemed the lodging of a Baker.

PETER giveth a beautiful Example of Ode-Writing.

THE CONTENTS OF THE ODE

His Majesty's Love for the Arts and Sciences, even in Quadrupeds – His Resolution to know the History of Brewing Beer – Billy Ramus sent Ambassador to Chiswell Street – Interview between Messers Ramus and Whitbread – Mr Whitbread's Bow, and Compliments to Majesty – Mr Ramus's Return from his Embassy – Mr Whitbread's Terrors described to Majesty by Mr Ramus – The King's Pleasure thereat – Description of People of Worship – Account of the Whitbread Preparation – The Royal Cavalcade to Chiswell Street – The Arrival at the Brewhouse – Great Joy of Mr Whitbread – His Majesty's Nod, the Queen's Dip, and a Number of Questions – The Marvellings of the Draymen described – His Majesty peepeth into a Pump – beautifully compared to a Magpie peeping into a Marrow-bone – The minute Curiosity of the King – Mr Whitbread endeavoureth to surprise Majesty – His Majesty puzzleth Mr Whitbread – Mr Whitbread's Horse expresseth Wonder – also Mr Whitbread's Dog – His Majesty maketh laudable Inquiry about Porter – Again puzzleth Mr Whitbread – King noteth *notable* Things – Profound Questions proposed by Majesty – As profoundly answered by Mr Whitbread – Majesty in a Mistake – Corrected by the Brewer – Majesty's Admiration of the Bell – Good Manners of the Bell – Fine Appearance of Mr Whitbread's Pigs – Majesty proposeth Questions, but benevolently waiteth not for Answers – Peter telleth the Duty of Kings – Discovereth one of his shrewd Maxims – Sublime Simile of a Waterspout and a King – The great Use of asking Questions – The Habitation of Truth – The Collation – The Wonders performed by the Royal Visitors – Majesty proposeth to take Leave – Offereth Knighthood to Mr Whitbread – Mr Whitbread's Objections – The King runneth a Rig on his Host – Mr Whitbread thanketh Majesty – Miss Whitbread curtseyeth – The Queen dippeth – The Cavalcade departeth.

Birth-day Ode

This day, this very day, gave birth
Not to the brightest Monarch upon earth,
 Because there are some brighter, and as big;
Who love the Arts that Men exalt to Heaven:
George loves them also, when they're given
 To four-legg'd Gentry, christened Dog and Pig,
Whose deeds in this our wonder-hunting Nation
Prove what a charming thing is education.

Full of the Art of Brewing Beer,
 The Monarch heard of Mister Whitbread's fame:
Quoth he unto the Queen, 'My dear, my dear,
 Whitbread hath got a marvellous great name.
Charly, we must, must, must see Whitbread brew;
Rich as us, Charly; richer than a Jew.
Shame, shame, we have not yet his Brewhouse seen.'—
Thus sweetly said the King unto the Queen.

Red-hot with Novelty's delightful rage,
To Mister Whitbread forth he sent a Page,
 To say that Majesty proposed to view,
With thirst of Knowledge deep inflamed,
His vats, and tubs, and hops, and hogsheads famed,
 And learn the noble secret, how to brew.

Of such undreamt of honour proud,
Most reverently the Brewer bow'd;
So humbly (so the humble story goes),
He touch'd e'en *terra firma* with his nose:
Then said unto the Page, hight Billy Ramus,
'Happy are we that our great King should name us,
As worthy unto Majesty to shew
How we poor Chiswell people brew.'

Away sprung Billy Ramus, quick as Thought:
To Majesty the welcome tidings brought;
 How Whitbread staring stood like any Stake,
And trembled: then the civil things he said:
On which the King did smile, and nod his head;
 For Monarchs like to see their Subjects quake.

Such horrors unto Kings most pleasant are,
    Proclaiming reverence and humility;
High thoughts too all those shaking fits declare
    Of kingly Grandeur and great Capability.
People of worship, wealth, and birth,
Look on the humbler Sons of Earth
    Indeed in a most humble light, God knows.
High Stations are like Dover's towering Cliffs,
Where Ships below appear like little Skiffs;
    The People walking on the strand, like Crows.

Muse, sing the stir that Mister Whitbread made;
Poor gentleman, most terribly afraid
    He should not charm enough his Guests divine:
He gave his Maids new aprons, gowns, and smocks;
And, lo! two hundred pounds were spent in frocks,
    To make th' Apprentices and Draymen fine.

Busy as Horses in a field of clover,
Dogs, cats, and chairs, and stools, were tumbled over,
Amidst the Whitbread rout of preparation
To treat the lofty Ruler of the Nation.

Now moved King, Queen, and Princesses, so grand,
To visit the first Brewer in the land;
Who sometimes swills his beer and grinds his meat
In a snug corner christen'd Chiswell-street;
But oftener, charm'd with fashionable air,
Amidst the gaudy Great of Portman-square....

Arrived, the King broad-grinn'd, and gave a nod
To Mister Whitbread; who, had God
    Come with his Angels to behold his beer,
With more respect he never could have met:
Indeed the man was in a sweat,
    So much the Brewer did the King revere.

Her Majesty contrived to make a dip:
Light as a Feather then the King did skip;
And ask'd a thousand Questions, with a laugh,
Before poor Whitbread comprehended half....

Thus was the Brewhouse fill'd with gabbling noise,
While Draymen, and the Brewer's Boys,
    Devoured the Questions that the King did ask:

In different parties were they staring seen,
Wondering to think they saw a King and Queen;
Behind a tub were some, and some behind a cask.

Some Draymen forced themselves (a pretty luncheon)
Into the mouth of many a gaping puncheon;
And through the bung-hole wink'd with curious eye,
To view, and be assured, what sort of things
Were Princesses, and Queens, and Kings,
For whose most lofty station thousands sigh.
And, lo! of all the gaping Puncheon clan,
Few were the Mouths that had not got a Man.

Now Majesty into a Pump so deep
Did with an opera-glass of Dollond peep,
Examining with care each wondrous matter
That brought up water.

Thus have I seen a Magpie in the street,
A chattering Bird we often meet,
A Bird for curiosity well known,
With head awry,
And cunning eye,
Peep knowingly into a Marrow-bone.

And now his curious Majesty did stoop,
To count the nails on every hoop;
And, lo! no single thing came in his way,
That, full of deep research, he did not say,
'What's this? hae, hae? what's that? what's this? what's that?'
So quick the words too, when he deign'd to speak,
As if each Syllable would break its Neck.

Thus, to the world of *great* while others crawl,
Our Sovereign peeps into the world of *small*:
Thus microscopic Geniuses explore
Things that too oft provoke the public scorn;
Yet swell of useful knowledges the store,
By finding Systems in a Pepper-corn.

Now Mister Whitbread serious did declare,
To make the Majesty of England stare,
That he had Butts enough, he knew,
Placed side by side, to reach along to Kew.
On which the King with wonder swiftly cried,

'What if they reach to Kew then side by side,
    What would they do, what, what, placed end to end?'
To whom, with knitted calculating brow,
The Man of Beer most solemnly did vow,
    Almost to Windsor that they would extend.
On which the King, with wondering mien,
Repeated it unto the wondering Queen.

On which, quick turning round his halter'd head,
The Brewer's Horse with face astonish'd neigh'd;
The Brewer's Dog too pour'd a note of thunder,
Rattled his chain, and wagg'd his tail for wonder.

Now did the King for other Beers inquire,
For Calvert's, Jordan's, Thrale's entire;
And, after talking of these different Beers,
Asked Whitbread if *his* Porter equall'd theirs.

This was a puzzling, disagreeing Question;
Grating like Arsenic on his Host's digestion:
A kind of question to the Man of Cask,
That not even Solomon himself would ask.

Now Majesty, alive to knowledge, took
A very pretty Memorandum-book,
With gilded leaves of asses' skin so white,
And in it legibly began to write:—

Memorandum

A charming place beneath the Grates,
For roasting Chestnuts or Potates.

Mem.

'Tis Hops that give a bitterness to Beer:
Hops grow in Kent, says Whitbread, and elsewhere.

Quaere

Is there no cheaper stuff? where doth it dwell?
Would not Horse-aloes bitter it as well?

Mem.

To try it soon on our Small-beer;
'Twill save us several pounds a year.

Mem.

To remember to forget to ask
Old Whitbread to my house one day.

Mem.

Not to forget to take of Beer the Cask,
The Brewer offer'd me, away.—

Now having pencil'd his Remarks so shrewd,
Sharp as the Point indeed of a new Pin;
His Majesty his watch most sagely view'd,
And then put up his asses' skin.

To Whitbread now deign'd Majesty to say,
'Whitbread, are all your Horses fond of Hay?'
'Yes, please your Majesty,' in humble notes
The Brewer answer'd: 'also, Sir, of Oats.
Another thing my Horses too maintains;
And that, an't please your Majesty, are Grains.'

'Grains, grains,' said Majesty, 'to fill their crops?
Grains, grains? That comes from hops; yes, hops, hops, hops.'

Here was the King, like Hounds sometimes, at fault.
'Sire,' cried the humble Brewer, 'give me leave
Your sacred Majesty to undeceive:
Grains, Sire, are never made from Hops, but Malt.'

'True,' said the cautious Monarch with a smile:
'From malt, malt, malt: I meant malt all the while.'—
'Yes,' with the sweetest bow rejoined the Brewer,
'An't please your Majesty, you did, I'm sure.'—
'Yes,' answered Majesty with quick reply,
'I did, I did, I did, I, I, I, I.'...

Now did the King admire the Bell so fine,
That daily asks the Draymen all to dine;
On which the Bell rung out (how very proper!)
To show it *was* a Bell, and had a Clapper.

And now before their Sovereign's curious eye,
Parents and Children, fine fat hopeful sprigs,
All snuffing, squinting, grunting, in their sty,
Appear'd the Brewer's tribe of handsome Pigs:
On which th' observant Man who fills a Throne,
Declared the Pigs were vastly like his own:

On which the Brewer, swallowed up in joys,
Tears and astonishment in both his eyes,
His soul brimful of sentiments so loyal,
Exclaimed: 'O Heavens! and can *my* Swine
Be deemed by Majesty so fine?
Heavens! can *my* Pigs compare, Sire, with Pigs Royal?'
To which the King assented with a nod:
On which the Brewer bowed, and said, 'Good God!'
Then wink'd significant on Miss,
Significant of wonder and of bliss;
Who, bridling in her chin divine,
Cross'd her fair hands, a dear old Maid,
And then her lowest curtsey made
For such high honour done her Father's Swine.

Now did his Majesty so gracious say
To Mister Whitbread, in his flying way,
'Whitbread, d'ye nick th'Excisemen now and then?
'Hae, Whitbread, when d'ye think to leave off trade?
Hae, what? Miss Whitbread's still a Maid, a Maid?
What, what's the matter with the Men?

'D'ye hunt? hae hunt? No, no, you are too old.
You'll be Lord May'r, Lord May'r one day;
Yes, yes, I've heard so; yes, yes, so I'm told:
Don't, don't the fine for Sheriff pay;
I'll prick you every year, man, I declare:
Yes, Whitbread, yes, yes; you shall be Lord May'r.

'Whitbread, d'ye keep a Coach, or job one, pray?
Job, job, that's cheapest; yes, that's best, that's best.
You put your liveries on the Draymen, hae?
Hae, Whitbread, you have feather'd well your nest.
What, what's the price now, hae, of all your stock?
But, Whitbread, what's o'clock, pray, what's o'clock?'

Now Whitbread inward said, 'May I be curst
If I know what to answer first';
Then search'd his brains with ruminating eye:
But ere the Man of Malt an answer found,
Quick on his heel, lo, Majesty turn'd round,
Skipp'd off, and baulk'd the pleasure of reply.—

Kings in inquisitiveness should be strong;
    From curiosity doth wisdom flow:
For 'tis a maxim I've adopted long,
    The more a man inquires, the more he'll know....

Now having well employed his Royal lungs
On nails, hoops, staves, pumps, barrels and their bungs,
The King and Co. sat down to a Collation
Of flesh, and fish, and fowl, of every Nation.

Dire was the clang of plates, of Knife and Fork,
That merciless fell like Tomahawks to work;
And fearless scalp'd the fowl, the fish, and cattle,
While Whitbread in the rear beheld the battle.

The conquering Monarch, stopping to take breath
Amidst the Regiments of Death,
    Now turn'd to Whitbread with complacence round,
And merry thus address'd the Man of Beer:
'Whitbread, is't true? I hear, I hear
    You're of an ancient family renown'd.
What, what? I'm told that you're a limb
Of Pym, the famous fellow Pym:
What, Whitbread, is it true what people say?
Son of a Roundhead are you? hae, hae, hae?

'I'm told that you send Bibles to your Votes,
    A snuffling Roundheaded Society;
Prayer-books, instead of Cash to buy them coats;
    Bunyans, and Practices of Piety:

'Your Bedford Votes would wish to change their fare;
Rather see Cash—yes, yes—than Books of Pray'r.
Thirtieth of January don't you feed?
Yes, yes; you eat Calf's Head, you eat Calf's Head.'

Now having wonders done on flesh, fowl, fish,
    Whole hosts o'erturn'd, and seized on all supplies;
The Royal Visitors express'd a wish
    To turn to House of Buckingham their eyes:

But first the Monarch, so polite,
Ask'd Mister Whitbread if he'd be a Knight.—
    Unwilling in the list to be enroll'd,
Whitbread contemplated the Knights of Peg,

Then to his generous Sovereign made a leg,
And said, he was afraid he was too old.
He thank'd however his most gracious King,
For offering to make him such a Thing....

Now from the table with Cesarean air
Up rose the Monarch with his laurel'd brow;
When Mister Whitbread, waiting on his chair,
Express'd much thanks, much joy, and made a Bow.

Miss Whitbread now so quick her Curtseys drops,
Thick as her honour'd Father's Kentish Hops:
Which hop-like curtseys were return'd by Dips
That never hurt the Royal knees and hips;
For hips and knees of Queens are sacred things,
That only bend on gala days
Before the Best of Kings,
When Odes of Triumph sound his praise.

Now through a thundering peal of kind Huzzas,
Proceeding some from hired and unhired jaws,
The Raree-show thought proper to retire;
While Whitbread and his Daughter fair
Survey'd all Chiswell-street with lofty air,
For, lo! they felt themselves some six feet higher....

Now God preserve all wonder-hunting Kings,
Whether at Windsor, Buckingham, or Kew-house;
And may they never do more foolish things
Than visiting Sam Whitbread and his Brewhouse!

Solomon and the Mouse-trap

A Man in rather an exalted station,
Whose eyes are always eyes of admiration;
Without distinction, fond of all things novel,
Even from the lofty Sceptre to the Shovel;
Just like stray'd Bullocks sauntering through the lanes,
Made frequent curiosity-campaigns:
Sometimes caught Grasshoppers; now, more profound,
Would sometimes find a Pin upon the ground;
Where if the head towards him happ'd to point,

His mind was wonderfully struck;
Indeed he felt a joy in every joint,
Because it always brings good luck.

This Gentleman, hight Solomon, one day
In quest of novelty pursued his way;
Like great Columbus, that famed navigator,
Who found the World we've lost across the water:
But rather on a somewhat narrow scale,
Lo! on dry land the Gentleman set sail.

That day it chanced to be his will,
To make discoveries at Salt-hill;
Where bounce he hopp'd into a Widow's house,
Whose hands were both employed so clever,
Doing their best endeavour
To catch that vile freebooter, Monsieur Mouse;
Whose death she oft did most devoutly pray for,
Because he ate the meat he could not pay for:

Resembling Christians in that saving trick;
Who, wanting to obtain good cheer,
Invented an ingenious scheme called *tick*,
That purchases, like Money, beef and beer.
Possess'd of *tick*, for cash men need not range,
Nor toil in taking or in giving change.

Eager did Solomon so curious clap
His rare round optics on the wondrous Trap
That did the duty of a Cat;
And, always fond of useful information,
Thus wisely spoke he with vociferation:
'What's that? what, what? Hae, hae! what's that?'
To whom replied the Mistress of the house,
'A Trap, an't please you, Sir, to catch a Mouse.'—

'Mouse! catch a mouse!' said Solomon with glee:
'Let's see, let's see; 'tis comical, let's see:
Mouse, mouse!' then pleased his eyes began to roll:
'Where, where doth he go in?' he marvelling cried.—
'There,' pointing to the hole, the Dame replied.—
'What, here?' cried Solomon, 'this hole, this hole?'

Then in he push'd his finger 'midst the wire;
That with such pains that finger did inspire,

He wish'd it out again with all his soul:
However, by a little squall and shaking,
He freed his finger from its piteous taking;
That is to say, he got it from the hole.

'What makes the Mouse, pray, go into the Trap?
Something,' he cried, 'that must his palate please?'
'Yes,' answer'd the fair Woman, 'Sir, a scrap
Of rusty bacon, or of toasted cheese.'—

'Oh, oh!' said Solomon, 'oh, oh! oh, oh!
Yes, yes, I see the meaning of it now:
The Mouse goes in, a rogue, to steal the meat,
Thinking to give his gums a pretty treat.'—
Then laugh'd he loudly, stretched his mouth a mile;
Which made the muscles of the Widow smile.

'Let's see, let's see,' cried Solomon; 'let's see:
Let me, let me, let me, let me, let me,'
Then took he up some Bacon, and did clap
A little slice so clever in the Trap.
Thus did he, by his own advice,
Induce himself to bait a Trap for Mice.

Now home he hied so nimbly, whelm'd with glory,
And told his Family the wondrous story
About the Widow's cheese and bacon scrap:
Nought suffer'd he to occupy his head,
Save mouse-ideas, till he went to bed;
Where blest he dreamt all night about the Trap.—...

Next day the Man of Wisdom came,
All glorious, to the house of this fair Dame,
To know if Master Mouse had smelt the bacon;
When, lo! to fill with joy his eager eyes,
And load those staring optics with surprise,
A real Mouse was absolutely taken....

Around the room the Mouse he bore,
Insulting the poor prisoner o'er and o'er;
Laughing and peeping through the wire,
As if his eyes and mouth would never tire.

How like to Tamerlane the Great,
Possess'd of most unlucky Bajazet,
	Who kept the vanquish'd Hero in a cage;
	Mock'd him before his mighty host,
With cruel names and threats, and grin and boast,
	And daily thus indulg'd Imperial rage!

Now o'er the Widow's Cat, poor watching Puss,
	He triumph'd too: and ask'd the Cat,
When *he* would act heroically thus;
	And if he dared to venture on a Rat.

To whom the Cat, as if in answer, mew'd;
	Which made the Man of Wisdom cry, 'Oh, oh!'
As if, with knowledge of Cat-speech endued,
	He thought that Puss had answered 'No.'
On which he laugh'd, and much enjoyed the joke;
Then told the Widow what the Cat had spoke.

Six days the Man of Wisdom went
Triumphant to Salt-hill, with big intent
	To catch the bacon-stealing Mouse:
Six Mice successively proclaim'd his art;
With which safe-pocketed he did depart,
	And show'd to all his much-astonish'd House.

But pleasures will not last for aye;
Witness the sequel of my Lay.
The Widow's vanity, her sex's flaw,
	Much like the vanity of other people
(A vapour, like the Blast that lifts a Straw
	As high, or higher, than Saint Martin's Steeple)—

This vanity then kidnapp'd her discretion,
	Design'd by God Almighty for her guard;
And of its purpose got the full completion,
	And all the Widow's future glories marr'd:

For, lo! by this same vanity impell'd,
	And to a middle-siz'd balloon,
With gas of consequence, sublimely swell'd,
	She burst with the important Secret soon.

Loud laugh'd the tickled people of Salt-hill:
    Loud laugh'd the merry Windsor folks around.
This was to Solomon an ugly pill:
    Her fatal error soon the Widow found;
For Solomon relinquish'd Mouse-campaign,
Nor deign'd to bait the Widow's Trap again.

Subject for Painters: Sir Joseph Banks and the Thief-takers

Sir Joseph, favourite of great Queens and Kings;
Whose wisdom, Weed and Insect Hunter sings,
    And Ladies fair applaud, with smile so dimpling;
Went forth one day, amidst the laughing fields,
Where Nature such exhaustless treasure yields,
    A simpling. . . .
Now did a Thief-taker so sly
Peep o'er a hedge with cunning eye,
    And quick espied the Knight with solemn air,
Deep in a ditch where water-cresses grow;
On which he to his Comrades cried, 'See, ho!'
    Then jump'd (unsportsman like) upon his hare.

Hare-like Sir Joseph did not squeak; but bawl'd,
With dread prodigiously appall'd.
    The Thief-takers no ceremony used;
But, taking poor Sir Joseph by the neck,
    They bade him speak:
But first with names their captive Knight abused.

'Sir, what d'ye take me for?' the Knight exclaim'd.—
    'A thief,' replied the Runners with a curse:
'And now, Sir, let us search you; and be damned!'
And then they search'd his pockets, fobs, and purse:

But 'stead of Pistol dire, and Crape,
    A pocket-handkerchief they cast their eye on,
Containing Frogs and Toads of various shape,
    Dock, Daisy, Nettletop, and Dandelion;
        To entertain, with great propriety,
            The Members of his sage Society.
Yet would not alter they their strong belief,
That this their Prisoner was a Thief.

'Sirs, I'm no highwayman,' exclaim'd the Knight.—
'No: there,' rejoin'd the Runners, 'you are right;
    A Footpad only; yes, we know your trade;
Yes, you're a pretty Babe of Grace:
We want no proofs, old Codger, but your face;
    So come along with us, old Blade.'

’Twas useless to resist, or to complain.
In vain Sir Joseph pleaded; ’twas in vain
That he was highly titled, that he swore:
The instant that poor Banks his titles counted,
Which to an *F. R. S.* and *Knight* amounted,
His Guardians laugh’d, and clapp’d, and cried ‘Encore!’

Sir Joseph told them, that a neighbouring Squire
Should answer for it that he was no thief:
On which they plumply damn’d him for a liar,
And said such stories should not save his beef;
And, if they understood their trade,
His mittimus would soon be made;
And forty pounds be theirs, a pretty sum,
For sending such a Rogue to Kingdom-come.

Now to the Squire moved Prisoner-knight and Co.:
The Runners taking him in tow;
Like Privateers of Britain’s warlike nation,
Towing a French East Indiaman, their prize,
So black, and of enormous size,
Safe into port for condemnation.

Whether they tied his hands behind his back,
For fear the Knight might run away,
And made, indelicate, his breeches slack,
We’ve no authority to say.

And now the Country People gather’d round,
And stared upon the Knight in thought profound,
Not on the system of Linnæus thinking;
Fancying they saw a rogue in every feature:—
Such is the Populace’s horrid nature
Towards people through misfortune sinking.

At length, amidst much Mob and mire,
Indeed amidst innumerable ranks,
Fatigued they reach the mansion of the Squire,
To prove th’identity of Joseph Banks.

Now to the Squire familiar bowed the Knight,
Who knew Sir Joseph at first sight
(What’s strongly mark’d, is quickly known again);
And, with a frown that awe and dread commanded,
The Thief-takers severely reprimanded
For thus mistaking Gentlemen:—

Then bade them ask a pardon on their knees,
    Of him that was a Knight and F. R. S.;
Who, rather than the higher powers displease,
    Imagined that they could not well do less.

Then on their knuckles raised they hands and eyes,
    And craved Sir Joseph's pardon, for belief
That when they jump'd upon him by surprise,
    They took so great a gemman for a thief;
Hoping to mind th'advice of godly books,
Viz. not to judge of people by their looks.

PETER illustrateth the Folly of Passion by a most apposite Tale.

The Knight and the Rats

A Knight lived in the West, not long ago;
Like Knights in general, not o'erwise, I trow.
This Knight's great Barn was visited by Rats;
In spite of poison, gins, and owls, and cats:
Like Millers, taking toll of the sweet corn,
Caroused they happily from night to morn.

Lo, waxing wroth, that neither gins nor cats,
Nor owls nor poison could destroy the Rats;
'I'll nab them by a scheme, by Heavens,' quoth he:
So of his neighbourhood he roused the mob,
Farmers and farmers' boys, to do this job;
His servants too of high and low degree;
And eke the tribes of dog, by sound of horn;
To kill the Rats that dared to taste the corn.

This done, the Knight, resolved with godlike ire,
Ran to his kitchen for a stick of fire,
From whence intrepid to the Barn he ran;
Much like the Macedonian, and fair Punk,
Who, at Persepolis so very drunk,
Did with their links the mighty ruin plan.

Now 'midst the dwelling flew the blazing stick:
Soon from the flames rush'd forth the Rats so thick;
Men, dogs, and bats, in furious war unite.
The conquer'd Rats lie sprawling on the ground;
The Knight, with eyes triumphant, stares around,
Surveys the carnage, and enjoys the sight.

Not even Achilles saw so blest his blade
Dismiss whole legions to th'infernal shade.
But, lo! at length, by this rat-driving flame,
Burnt was the corn; the walls down thundering came;
The meaning of it was not far to learn:
When, turning up those Billiard-balls his Eyes,
That held a pretty portion of surprise,
'Zounds, what a blockhead! I have burnt the barn.'

An Apology for Kings: Story the Second

From Salisbury Church to Wilton House, so grand,
Return'd the mighty Ruler of the Land.
'My Lord, you've got fine Statues,' said the King.—
'A Few, beneath your Royal notice, Sir.'
Replied Lord Pembroke.—'Stir, my Lord, stir, stir;
Let's see them all, all, all, all, every thing.

'Who's this? who's this? who's this fine fellow here?'—
'Sesostris,' bowing low, replied the Peer.—
'*Sir Sostris*, hey? *Sir Sostris?* 'pon my word!
Knight or a Baronet, my Lord?
One of my making? what, my lord? *my making?*'—
This, with a vengeance, was mistaking!

'*Se*sostris, Sire," so *soft*, the Peer replied;
'A famous King of Egypt, Sir, of old.'—
'Poh, poh!' th'instructed Monarch snappish cried,
'I need not *that*, I need not *that*, be told.

'Pray, pray, my Lord, who's that big fellow there?'—
' 'Tis Hercules,' replies the shrinking Peer.—
'Strong fellow, hey, my Lord? strong fellow, hey?
Clean'd stables; crack'd a Lion like a Flea;
Kill'd Snakes, great Snakes, that in a cradle found him.—
The Queen, Queen's coming: wrap an apron round him.'

PETER adviseth to read Esop's Fables.

The Frogs and Jupiter

The Frogs so happy, 'midst their peaceful pond,
Of emperors grew at once extremely fond;
Yes, yes, an emperor was a glorious thing:
Each really took it in his addle pate,
'Twould be so charming to exchange their state!
An emperor would such heaps of blisses bring!

Sudden out hopp'd the Nation on the grass,
Frog-man and yellow Wife, and Youth and Lass,
A numerous tribe, to knuckle down to Jove,
And pray the God to send an emperor down;
'Twas such a pretty thing, th'Imperial Crown!
So form'd their pleasures, honours, to improve!

Forth from his old blue Weather-box, the Skies,
Jove briskly stepp'd, with two wide-wondering eyes:
'Mynheers,' quoth Jove, 'if ye are wise, be quiet;
Know when you're happy."—But he preach'd in vain;
They made the most abominable riot:
'An Emperor, Emperor, yes, we *must* obtain.'—

'Well, *take* one,' cried the God; and down he swopp'd
A monstrous Piece of Wood, from whence he chopp'd
Kings for the gentlefolks of ancient days:
Stunn'd at the sound, the Frogs all shook with dread;
Like Dab-chicks, under water push'd each head,
Afraid a single nose so pale to raise.

At length one stole a peep, and then a second,
Who, slily winking, to a third Frog beckon'd;
And so on, till they all obtain'd a peep.
Now nearer, nearer, edging on they drew;
And finding nothing terrible, nor new,
Bold on his Majesty began to leap:

Such hopping this way, that way, off and on!
Such croaking, laughing, ridiculing, fun!

In short, so very shameful were they grown,
So much of grace and manners did they lack,
One little Villain saucily squat down,
And, with a grin, defiled the Royal back.

Now unto Jove they kneeling pray'd again:
    'O Jupiter, this is so sad a beast,
So dull a Monarch, so devoid of brain!
    Give us a King of spirit, Jove, at least.'

The God complied, and sent them Emperor Stork,
Who with his loving Subjects went to work;
Chased the poor sprawling imps from pool to pool,
Resolv'd to get a handsome bellyful.

Now gasping, wedged within his iron beak,
Did wriggling scores most lamentably squeak:
Bold push'd the Emperor on, with stride so noble,
Bolting his Subjects with majestic gobble.

Again the croaking tribe began to pray,
'Midst hoppings, scramblings, murder, and dismay:
'Oh save us, Jove, from this inhuman Turk!
Oh save us from this Imp of Hell!'—
'Mynheers,' quoth Jove, 'pray keep your Emperor Stork:
Fools never know when they are *well*.'

Pleasure's a lass that will at length prevail:
Witness the little pleasant following Tale:—

Old Simon

Narcissa, full of grace, and youth, and charms,
Had slept some years in good Old Simon's arms;
Her kind and lawful Spouse, that is to say:
Who, following of numbers the example,
Wishing of sweet young Flesh to have a sample,
Married this charming Girl upon a day.

For from grey-headed men, and thin, and old,
Young Flesh is finely form'd to keep the cold.
Thus of the pretty Shunammite we read,
Who warm'd the good King David and his bed,
Brought back his flagging spirits all so cool,
And kept the King of Israel warm as wool.
Indeed she warmer could the Monarch keep,
Than any thing belonging to a Sheep.

Most virtuous was Narcissa, lo!
All purity from top to toe;
As Hebe sweet, and as Diana chaste.
None but Old Simon was allowed to kiss,
Though hungry as a Hound to snap the bliss;
Nor squeeze her hand, nor take her round the waist.

Had any dared to give her a green gown,
The Fair had petrified him with a frown:
For chastity, Lord bless us! is *so* nice;
Pure as the Snow, and colder than the Ice.

Thus then, as I have said before,
Sweetly she slept, and probably might snore,
In good Old Simon's unmolesting arms.
Some years, with this *antique* of christian clay,
Did pass in this same tasteless, tranquil way:
Ah, Gods, how lucky for such tender charms!

Yes, very fortunate it seem'd to be;
For, had Narcissa wedded some young chaps,
Their impudences, all forsooth so free,
Had robb'd her eyes by night of half their naps.

And yet, on second thoughts (sometimes the best),
Ladies might choose to lose a little rest,
Keep their eyes open for a Lover's sake,
And thus a sacrifice to Cupid make.

It pleased at length the Lord who dwells on high,
To bid the good old simple Simon die;
 'Sleep with his fathers,' as the Scripture has it;
Narcissa wept, that they were doom'd to part,
Blubber'd and almost broke her little heart;
 So great her grief, that nothing could surpass it.
Not Niobe mourn'd more for fourteen Brats;
Nor Mistress Tofts, to leave her twenty Cats.

Not to his grave was poor Old Simon hurried;
No! 'twas a fortnight full ere he was buried.
 'Tis said, Old Simon verily did stink.
A pretty Sermon on th'occasion given,
Prov'd his good works, and that he was in heaven;
 Scraps too of Latin did the parson link
Unto the Funeral Sermon, all so sweet,
The Congregation and the Dead to greet:

For every Wife that is genteely bred,
Orders a sprig of Latin for the dead.
And of a sprig of Latin what's the cost?—
A poor Half-guinea at the most.

Latin sounds well: it is a kind of Balm,
That honoureth a corpse just like a Psalm;
And 'tis believed by folks of pious qualm,
Heaven won't receive a Soul without a Psalm.—

But now for poor Narcissa, wailing Dove!
Nothing, no, nothing equall'd her dear love;
 Such tears and groans burst forth, from eyes and mouth;
Where'er she went, she was so full of woes,
Just like a dismal Day that rains and blows
 From every quarter, east, west, north and south;
And like some Fountains were Narcissa's Eyes,
Lifting a constant water to the skies.

Resolved to keep his Image near her breast,
 She got him beautifully carved in wood;
Made it her Bed-fellow, to sooth her rest;

And thought him much like him of flesh and blood,
Because it lay so wonderfully quiet,
And, like Old Simon, never bred a riot.
'Twas for some weeks, sweet soul! her pious plan,
Nightly to hug her dear old wooden Man.

Yet, verily, it doth my fancy strike,
That buxom Widows, full of rich desires,
Full of fine prancing blood, and Love's bright fires,
Might such a wooden Supplement dislike.
But who can answer for the Sex indeed?
Of things most wonderful we sometimes read!

It came to pass, a Youth admired the Dame;
Burning to satisfy a lawless flame;
With much more Passion fill'd, the rogue, than Grace.—
What did he? Bribed, one night, Narcissa's Maid,
And got his limbs, so devilish saucy, laid
(Th'imposters!) in poor wooden Simon's place.
Susan, though born among a vulgar tribe,
Knew nature, and the nature of a Bribe.—

The Dame came up, delicious, and undrest;
When Susan's candle suddenly went out.
Misfortunes sometimes will attend the best:
No matter; sweet Narcissa made no rout.
She could not miss the way, although 'twas dark,
Unto her bed, and dear old Bit of Bark.

In slipp'd the Fair, so fresh, beneath the sheets,
Thinking to hug her dear old oaken Love:
But, lo, her Bed-fellow with kisses greets:
She trembles like an Aspen, pretty Dove!
In short, her terror kept her so much under,
She could not get away; and where's the wonder?
Since 'tis an old and philosophic notion,
That terror robbeth all the limbs of motion.

The upshot of the matter soon was this:
Her horrors sunk, and died, at every kiss;
And, 'stead of wishing for the Man of Wood,
She seem'd to relish that of Flesh and Blood

Next day, but not indeed extremely soon
(Some five or six o'clock, the afternoon),

Susan came tapping at the chamber door:—
(Now this was very prudent, to be sure;
    It had been foolish to have tapped till then:)
'Well, Madam, what d'ye choose for dinner, pray?'—
'Fish, flesh, and fowl,' the Lady quick did say:
    'The best of everything; I don't care when.'—

'But, Madam, I want wood to make a fire:
    'Tis rather late; our hands we have no time on.'—
'Oh!' cried Narcissa, full of her new Squire,
    'Then, Susan you may go and burn Old Simon.'

Ladies and gemmen, the Widow of Ephesus. Silence.

The Widow of Ephesus

A Tale

At Ephesus (a handsome town of Greece)
There lived a Lady, a most lovely piece;
 In short, the charming Toast of all the town.
In wedlock's velvet bonds had lived the Dame:
Yes, brightly did the torch of Hymen flame;
 When Death, too cruel, knock'd her Husband down.

This was indeed a lamentable stroke:
Prudentia's gentle heart was nearly broke;
 Tears pea-like trickle, shrieks her face deform;
Sighs, sighs succeeding, leave her snowy breast;
Winds, call'd hysterical, expand her chest,
 As though she really had devour'd a storm.

Now, fainting, calls she on her poor dead love:
How like the wailings of the widow'd Dove!

All Ephesus upon the wonder gazed:
Men, women, children, really were amazed.
'Tis true, a few Old Maids abused the pother:
'Heavens! if *one* Husband dies, why, take *another*,'
 Said they, contemptuous cocking up the nose:
'Ridiculous enough! and what about?
To make for a dead husband such a rout!
 There are as fine as he, one might suppose.

'A body would presume, by grief so mad,
Another Husband was not to be had.
But men are not so very scarce, indeed:
More than are good, there are; God mend the breed!'

Such was the conversation of Old Maids,
Upon this Husband's visit to the shades.

At length her Spouse was carried to the tomb,
Where poor Prudentia moped amid the gloom.

 One little lamp, with solitary beam,
Show'd the dark coffin that contain'd her dear;
And gave a beauteous sparkle to each Tear,
 That rill-like dropp'd, or rather like a stream.

Resolv'd was she, amid this tomb to sigh;
To weep, and wail, and groan, and starve, and die:
    No comfort, no; no comfort would she take
Her friends beheld her anguish with great pain,
Begg'd her to try amusement; but in vain:
    'No; she would perish, perish for his sake.'

Her flaxen tresses all dishevell'd flow'd,
Her vestments loose, her tucker all abroad,
    Revealing such fair swelling orbs of woe!
Her lids, in swimming grief, now look'd on high,
Now downward droop'd; and now she pour'd a sigh
    (How tuneful!) on her dear pale Spouse below.

Who would not covet death, for such sweet sighs;
To be bewail'd by such a pair of eyes?

It happen'd that a Rogue, condemn'd to death,
Resign'd (to please the law) his roguish breath;
        And near the vault did this same Felon swing:
For fear the Rogue's relations, or a friend,
Might steal him from the rope's disgraceful end,
    A smart young Soldier watch'd the Thief and string.

This Son of Mars, upon his silent station,
Hearing, at night, a dismal lamentation,
    Stole to the place of woe; that is, the tomb:
And, peeping in, beheld a beauteous face
That look'd with such a charming tragic grace,
    Displaying sorrow for a Husband's doom.

The Youth most naturally express'd surprise,
And scarcely could he credit his two eyes:
'God God, Ma'am! pray, Ma'am, what's the matter here?
    Sweet Ma'am, be comforted; you must, you shall:
    At times misfortunes, even the *best* befall.
Pray stop your grief, Ma'am; save that precious tear.'—

'Go, Soldier, leave me," sighed the Fair again,
In such a melting melancholy strain,
    Casting her eyes of woe upon the Youth:
'I cannot, will not, live without my Love!'
And then she threw her glistening eyes above,
That swam in tears of constancy and truth.

'Madam,' rejoin'd the Youth, and press'd her hand,
'Indeed you shall not my advice withstand;
For Heaven's sake don't stay here, to weep and howl:
Pray take refreshment.'—Off at once he set,
And quickly brought the mourner drink and meat;
A bottle of Madeira and a fowl.
And bread and beer,
Her heart to cheer.

'Ah! gentle Youth, you bid me eat in vain;
Leave me, oh, leave me, Soldier, to complain:
Yes, sympathizing Youth withdraw your wine.
My sighs and tears shall be my only food:
Thou knewest not my Husband kind and good,
For whom this heart shall ever, ever pine.'

And then she cast upon the Youth an eye
All tender, saying, 'Soldier, let me die.'
And then she press'd his hand, with friendship warm.—
'You shall not die, by Heaven!' the Soldier swore:
'No, to the World such beauty I'll restore,
And give it back again its only charm.'

Such was th'effect of her delicious Hand,
That charm'd his senses like a Wizard's Wand.

'What! howl for ever for a breathless *clod*!
Ma'am, you shall eat a leg of fowl, by God.'

With that he clapp'd wine, fowl, bread, beer and all,
Without more ceremony, on the pall.

'Well, Soldier, if you do insist,' quoth she,
All in a saint-like, sweet, complying tone,
'I'll try if Grief will let me pick a bone.
Your health, Sir.'—'Thank you kindly, Ma'am,' quoth he.

As grief absorbs the senses, the fair Dame
Scarce knew that she was eating, or yet drinking;
So hard is it a roaring grief to tame,
And keep the sighing pensive soul from thinking:—

So that the fowl and wine soon pass'd indeed;
Quickly away too stole the beer and bread,
All down her pretty little swelling throat.—

And now, whate'er Philosophers may think,
Sorrow is much obliged to meat and drink,
Whose soothing virtues stop the plaintive note;
And, says the anatomic art,
'The stomach's very near the heart.'

Prudentia found it so: a gentler sigh
Stole from her lovely breast; a smaller tear,
Containing less of anguish, did appear
Within the pretty corner of her eye;
Her eye's dark Cloud dispersing too apace
(Just like a Cloud that oft conceals the Moon),
Let out a brighter lustre o'er her face,
Seeming to indicate dry weather soon.

Her tongue too somewhat lost its mournful style;
Her rosebud-lips expanded with a smile:
Which pleased the gallant Soldier, to be sure,
Happy to think he saved the Dame from Death;
Yes, from his hug preserved the sweetest breath,
And to a wounded heart prescribed a cure.

Mow Mars's Son a minute left the Dame,
To see if all went well with Rogue and rope;
But, ere he to the fatal gibbet came,
The Knave had deem'd it proper to elope.

In short, attendance on the Lady's grief
Had lost him his Companion, the hang'd Thief,
Whose friends had kindly filch'd him from the string.
Quick to the Lady did the Soldier run:
'Madam, I shall be hang'd, as sure's a gun:
O Lord! the Thief's gone off, and *I* shall swing.

'Madam, it was the Royal declaration,
That if the Rogue was carried off
(Whether by *soft* means or by *rough*,
No matter), *I* should take his situation.
'O Lord, O Lord! my fate's decreed:
O Ma'am! I shall be hang'd indeed.

'O Lord, O Lord! this comes of creeping
To graves and tombs; this comes of peeping;
This is th'effect of running from my duty.

Oh curse my folly! What an ape
Was I, to let the Thief escape!
    This comes of fowl, and wine, and beer, and beauty.

'Yet, Ma'am, I beg your pardon, too;
Since if I'm hang'd, 'twill be for you.'—

'Cheer up, my gallant Friend,' replied the Dame,
    Squeezing his hand, and smoothing down his face:
'No, no, you sha'nt be hang'd, nor come to shame;
    My husband here shall take the fellow's place:
Nought but a lump of clay can *he* be counted,
Then let him mount:'—and lo! the Corpse was mounted;
Made a good Thief; nay, so complete,
The people never smelt the cheat.

Now from the gibbet to the tomb again
    Haste, arm in arm, the Soldier and the Fair;
T'exchange for kisses, and the turtle's strain,
    Sad hymns of death and ditties of despair.

Pindariana: Ode to Two Mice in a Trap

So, Sir and Madam! you at length are taken,
After your dances over cheese and bacon,
  And tasting every dainty in your way?
Now to my question answer, if ye please:
Speak, did ye *make* the bacon or the cheese?
  What sort of a defence d'ye set up, pray?

Thus at free cost to breakfast, dine, and sup!
Even mild Judge Buller ought to hang you up,
  So full of the sweet milk of human nature.
What sort of fate, young People, should ye choose?
In purling Strems your pretty mouths amuse;
  Or feed the Cat's fond jaws, that for you water?

I see ye are two Lovers, by your eyes;
I hear ye are two Lovers, by your sighs:
  But what avail your looks, or what avail
Your sighs so soft, or what indeed your tears,
Or what your parting agonies and fears;
  Since Death must pay a visit to your jail?

Ay, you may kiss and pant, and pant and kiss,
  And put your pretty noses through the wire:
Ay, peep away, sweet Sir, and gentle Miss;
  No more the Moon shall mark your amorous fire
Around the loaded pantry pour the ray,
And guide your gambols with her silver day.

Your prison-door now, Culprits, let me ope.—
Now, now! You're *off*! it is a lucky hop.
  Ye're in the right on't, nimble Nymph and Swain.
Go, rogues; but if once more I catch you here—
What then?—What *then*! why then, I strongly fear,
  Ye little robbers, you'll escape again.

Ode on the Choleric Character

Happy the man whose heart of such a sort is,
As holds more Buttermilk than Aqua-fortis:
    But, Lord! how passionate are certain folk!
How like the Sea, reflecting every form,
So placid; the next instant in a storm,
    Dashing against the inoffensive rock;

Mounting towards the skies with such a thunder,
As though it wish'd (the leveller!) to bring under
Sun, moon, and stars, and tear them into tatters!—
Such passions verily are serious matters.

Men in morality should ne'er be idle,
But for those passions make a strong curb-bridle.

When lofty Man doth quarrel with a Pin,
In *man* resides the folly or the sin;
Not in the brass, by which his finger's spitted:
For with a small philosophy we find,
That, as a Pin is not endowed with mind,
    Of malice call'd *prepense* Pin stands acquitted.

Thus then, his awkwardness must bear the blame;
And thus, to persecute the Pin's a shame.

Many inanimates, as well as Pins,
Suffer for others' fooleries and sins.

How oft a drunken blockhead damns a Post,
    That overturns him, breaks his shins or head;
Whose eyes should certainly have viewed the coast,
    And have avoided this same Post so dread:
Whereas he should have spread his idle cries,
And only damn'd his own two blinking eyes.

PETER Telleth a Tale of THE TOPER AND THE FLIES.

A group of Topers at a table sat,
    With Punch that much regales the thirsty soul:
Flies soon the party joined, and joined the chat;
    Humming and pitching round the mantling Bowl.

At length those Flies got drunk, and, for their sin,
Some hundreds lost their legs, and tumbled in;
And, sprawling 'midst the Gulf profound,
Like Pharaoh and his daring host, were drown'd.

Wanting to drink, one of the Men
Dipp'd from the Bowl the drunken host,
And drank; then, taking care that none were lost,
He put in every mother's son agen.

Up jump'd the Bacchanalian Crew on this,
Taking it very much amiss;
Swearing, and in the attitude to smite.
'Lord!' cried the man, with gravely lifted eyes,
'Though *I* don't like to swallow Flies,
I did not know but others might.'

Ballade: To a Fish of the Brooke

Why flyest thou away, with fear?
Trust me, there's nought of danger near;
  I have no wicked hooke,
All cover'd with a snaring bait,
Alas! to tempt thee to thy fate,
  And dragge thee from the brooke.

O harmless Tenant of the Flood,
I do not wish to spill thy blood;
  For nature unto thee
Perchance hath given a tender wife,
And children dear, to charme thy life,
  As she hath done for me.

Enjoy thy streame, O harmless Fish!
And when an Angler, for his dish,
  Through gluttony's vile sin,
Attempts, a wretch, to pull thee out;
God give thee strength, O gentle Trout,
  To pull the raskal in!

The Young Crows and the Young Wrens

A Crow upon a lofty tree
  Did build her sticky nest;
And Younglings did she bring to light,
  In number five at least.

One morning, on a summer's day,
  Did peep each youngling Crow,
And spied upon a brambling-bush
  Some youngling Wrens below.

These simple Wrens in happy glee
  Did spread their little wing;
And, lightsome, hopp'd from bush to bush,
  And merrily did sing.

'Poor humble creatures!' cried the Crows;
  'Each is a beggar wight:
Look up to us, and see our state;
  Our house's lofty height.

'We look into the beamy skies,
While you through hedges wade:
We gaze upon the morning sun,
While ye are lost in shade.

'Poor imps, depart, nor here offend;
Take off each silly face:
This hill was only made for Crows;
Then do not us disgrace.

'If you do not this region quit,
We'll dung upon you soon.'—
The smiling Wrens made answer none,
But trill'd their little tune.

Short time had pass'd, when suddenly
Grim Boreas 'gan howl;
The thunder crack'd, the lightning flash'd,
And frighted Man and Fowl.

While thus the dreadful thunder crack'd,
And lightning broad did flash;
The limb whereon the Crows were perch'd
Did give a sudden crash.

Down came the limb, and with it down
Did tumble each young Crow:
Some broke their legs, and some their wings,
And doleful look'd below.

'Twas now the time for Wrens to jeer;
So forth did fly the train,
And, twittering, saw with smiles the Crows
All sprawling on the plain.

Then taunting, an arch Wren began:
'Sir Crows, of high renown,
Ye came, by this your dirty trim,
All in a hurry down:—

'And by the look of all your limbs,
And feathers sous'd with rain,
It will be some small time before
Your graces mount again.

'Proud fools, how silly ye descend
From skies to dirty fens!
Thank Heaven, with hedges we're content,
And happy to be wrens.'

Hymn to Adversity

Thus sung the Bard of old, and deem'd no fool,
'Sweet are the uses of adversity;'
A Dame who kicketh from your rump your stool,
And, savage, showeth not one grain of mercy t'ye;
Bids all your fancied-dearest friends turn tail;
Greets with wired whips, and blesses with a jail.

O Mistress of this wisdom-teaching pain,
With Pillory, Gibbet, Famine, in thy train,
Go knock, God bless thee, knock at others' doors.
By all my favourite Gods of Prose and Rhyme,
I feel not thy philosophy sublime:
Go, seek the zealot who thy stripes implores....

My taste is dull; yes, vastly dull indeed:
I hate to see a brother-mortal bleed.
I hate to hear a gentle nature groan;
And, Goddess, more especially my own....

Thou possibly mayst be a good physician,
But *certes* dost not know my weak condition.
Blisters, and scarifying, and spare diet,
Would set my nervous system in a riot...
Thine 'iron scourge' would really act in vain,
So apt am I to make wry mouths at pain;
At disappointment much inclined to moan.
Whenever then, O Goddess, things we see
That with one's nature so much disagree,
Methinks 'twere better they were let alone.

To tumble from a house, or from a tow'r,
And break a luckless brace of legs and arms,
Would make one look most miserably sour:—
Yet there are men who deem all these no harms.

Then seek them, Goddess; souse them on the stones;
And, for their goodly comfort, crack their bones.

If in a well-stuff'd coach, well-overset,
A broken leg and thigh and arm I get,
    I am not, I confess, of that pure leaven,
To crawl out on my hands and knees, and say,
Grace-like, 'For what I have received this day,
    I humbly thank thee, O most gracious Heaven!'

O Mistress of the terrifying mien,
    The boatswain's deep-toned voice and brawny arm,
Oh be not within leagues of Peter seen!
    Thy cat-o'-nine-tails cannot, cannot charm.
A stupid Scholar, Goddess, I shall be:
Thy conversations are too deep for me....

Besides, 'tis late, O Goddess, in the day;
I'm not a subject fit for thee to flay:
    To speak the truth, my nerves too nicely feel.
Go, search the motley mixture of mankind;
Some young enthusiast wild thou soon mayst find,
    Proud of thy whips, and glad to grace thy wheel.

So great for my own person is my love,
    And hard thy lessons, I can't now begin 'em.—
Besides, as I have hinted just above,
    I'd rather read of battles than be in 'em.

The Poet remarks the different Treatment of Bards of the present, and that of past Ages; and complains of not meeting as much Encouragement for his Verses as Organ-grinders, Exhibitors of Bears, Camels, Dancing Dogs, and Punch.

Elegy

In days of yore, the golden days of Rhyme,
    The mighty Monarch to his Minstrel bow'd;
But what is now the character sublime?
    A blind old Ballad-singer and his crowd.

Kings too were Poets: David to his Lyre
    Sung sweetest elegy; and David's Son
Sung to the Harp with all his Father's fire,
    And all the Virgins of Judea won.

And thou, Isaiah, too didst deal in Song;
    Born, let me say, a gentleman, and bred:
In satire, let me tell thee, rather strong;
    That broke the Babylonian Monarch's head.

Had I said half as bad of George the Third,
    As thou of Babylon's imperious King,
My fate had been far different, take my word;
    My just reward, the pillory or the string.

The Organ-grinding Girl, whose discords kill,
    Is beckon'd by our Dames of highest Quality:
And grist she gaineth to her screaming mill;
    And, curtseying, thanks them for their hospitality.

To me no Lover of the Muses cries,
    'Out with thy wallet, let us hear thy Odes;
Then George's image shall delight thine eyes:
    Behold, a sixpence for the Song of Gods.'

No Nymph of Quality on Peter calls;
    No Lesbia, fond of sparrows and the dove;
And bid me make them melting Madrigals;
    And say, 'Sweet Peter, sing us songs of love.'

The Man who carries Punch about the streets,
    His scolding Wife, the Baker, and the Devil;
With fair rewards from all spectators meets,
    And to his poverty each purse is civil.

The Man who leads his Camel up and down,
    Where sports a grinning Monkey on his hump;
Dines princely, such the favour of the Town;
    And never mourns, like me, in doleful dump.

The Men who lead about a Dancing Bear,
    Or Dancing Dogs, good living never lack;
While *I*, who lead the Muses, (fate severe!)
    Can neither treat my belly nor my back.

The Clowns of thirty pounds a year (no more),
    Laugh at the Sons of Song, and scornful pass us:
'One little rood of dirty land,' they roar,
    'Is worth a thousand acres of Parnassus.'